Theological Reflections

⌘⌘⌘⌘⌘⌘

Meditations on Faith & Reason

⌘⌘⌘⌘⌘⌘

Presented by the Faculties of
Cleveland St. Mary Seminary and Borromeo Seminary:

Rev. Mark Latcovich   Rev. Joseph Koopman   Rev. Mark Hollis
Rev. Gerald Bednar   Rev. Lawrence Tosco, CSJ   Rev. John Loya
Dr. Chad Engelland   Rev. Michael McCandless   Rev. Mark Ott
Rev. Damian Ference   Sr. Mary McCormick, OSU   Dr. Edward Kaczuk
Rev. Michael Woost   Rev. Francis Moloney, SDB   Rev. Andrew Turner

ೞೞೞೞ

Edited by
Rev. Gerald J. Bednar, Ph.D.

ೞೞೞೞ

A St. Mary Seminary
Pastoral Publication

SMS Publications
Wickliffe, Ohio

2014

SMS Publications
28700 Euclid Ave.
Wickliffe, OH 44092

Nihil Obstat: Father John G. Vrana, STD
                     Censor Deputatus

Imprimatur: +Most Reverend Richard G. Lennon, MTh, MA
                     Bishop of Cleveland

Given at Cleveland, Ohio, on 9 May 2014.

The *Nihil Obstat* and *Imprimatur* are official declarations that a book or pamphlet is free of doctrinal or moral error. No implication is contained therein that those who have granted the *Nihil Obstat* and *Imprimatur* agree with the contents, opinions or statements expressed.

Dedication

This volume is dedicated to all the graduates of Cleveland St. Mary and Borromeo Seminaries, all the past faculty members who have taught in their formation programs, and, most of all, to the people of the Diocese of Cleveland whose constant support has ensured the continued operation of St. Mary Seminary throughout the past 165 years, and Borromeo Seminary throughout the past 60 years.

Table of Contents

Preface

At the start of the 2013-2014 academic year, Saint Mary Seminary and Graduate School of Theology began its 165th year of faithful service to the Diocese of Cleveland. I am honored to lead this fine institution in addition to the undergraduate formation program at Borromeo Seminary which will celebrate its 60th year of operation at the beginning of the 2014-2015 academic year.

It is in commemoration of those anniversaries that this volume has been produced and is presented to the people of the Diocese of Cleveland, the Seminary graduates and the faculty who served throughout the years of the seminaries' existence.

Together these two seminaries have provided first-class formation programs to prepare priests for the Diocese. The faculties who serve these seminaries are dedicated men and women who instruct the seminarians in Scripture, philosophy, theology, ethics, liturgy, spirituality, pastoral skills, and history. They also provide trusted guidance for the pastoral development, human formation and spiritual discernment that seminarians must experience during their formation.

In 1999, Dennis Sadowski, the then-Editor of the Diocesan newspaper, *The Universe Bulletin*, asked faculty members at the seminaries to write an ongoing column concerning theological topics for its readers. They responded with creativity and grace. Faculty members wrote, on a rotating basis, columns dealing with their theological specialties and particular interests. The column was called "Theologically Speaking," and has run in the newspaper for the past 15 years.

This volume represents a compilation of some of the articles that have appeared in that column. Faculty members submitted writings that they thought would appeal to a wide readership. I sincerely hope you enjoy browsing through the book and reading those articles that catch your interest.

I would like to thank Joe Polito, the Chief Executive Officer, President and Associate Publisher of *The Universe Bulletin*, and Nancy Erikson, its Editor, for their support for this project. Finally, I would like to thank Fr. Jerry Bednar, the Vice-President and Vice-Rector of St. Mary Seminary, for suggesting this volume, editing it, and seeing it through to its completion.

May the insights you gain through these articles truly benefit your faith and your devotion in living our Catholic faith.

Rev. Mark A. Latcovich, Ph.D.
President/Rector
St. Mary Seminary and Graduate School of Theology
and
Borromeo Seminary

Introduction

The purpose of this volume is three-fold. First, it commemorates the anniversaries of two seminaries that have contributed greatly to the life of the Diocese of Cleveland. Second, it serves as a sort of time capsule that collects a sampling of work done by current faculty members who have contributed articles to *The Universe Bulletin's* "Theologically Speaking" column since 1999. As such, these chapters convey some of the faculty's thoughts and interests presented in a pastoral setting. Third, this book offers readers an opportunity to consider various theological and religious issues presented in a short, convenient, and accessible format. It assumes no prior theological training, nor does it require the reader to follow the chapters in any particular sequence. The bite-sized chapters do not require any significant commitment of time or energy, but just might spark further interest in a topic.

There is something here for everyone. If some readers need reassurance in some of the time-honored truths that Catholics hold dear, this volume presents articles that can reaffirm those truths with renewed conviction. If other readers feel the need to be challenged in their understanding of the faith, several articles will show them new avenues that the typical lay person rarely explores. If other readers would like to investigate different aspects of spirituality, a number of articles can plant the seeds of serenity and prayer in their lives. If still others would like to consider vocations, several chapters offer guidance, encouragement and strategies to approach the issue.

A couple of observations might help to explain the contents and organization of this commemorative anthology.

First of all, faculty members were asked simply to submit a few of their "Theologically Speaking" newspaper articles that they would like to see published in this volume. No restraints were placed on topic selection, nor was any effort made to solicit designated topics from particular members of the faculty. As a result, some of the articles relate more closely to their section topics than others. I have grouped the chapters into seven sections: (1) Biblical Matters; (2) The Splendor of the Human; (3) The Summertime of the Soul; (4) Spirituality; (5) Liturgical Life; (6) Life, Death and Morals Along the Way; and (7) Hearing the Call: Vocations. Hopefully the categories will be descriptive enough for readers to navigate their way to areas of interest.

Secondly, special attention should be given to the very first chapter written by Rev. Francis J. Moloney, SDB, of the Australian Catholic University. A preeminent Biblical scholar who served on the International Theological Commission for 18 years, Fr. Moloney has gained worldwide notoriety, especially for his work on the Gospel of John. St. Mary Seminary was honored to host him as its 2013 Mullen Lecturer. Father Moloney also became the first Mullen Scholar in Residence, and, as such, he taught a course at St. Mary Seminary on the Gospel of Mark during the Fall of 2013. Universally loved and admired, Fr. Moloney shared himself most generously, not only at the Seminary, but at various parishes where he both celebrated Mass and lectured during his stay. I asked Fr. Moloney to submit a chapter since he was so much a part of the faculty during the 2013-2014 academic year. His response was immediate and gracious.

Let me give you a roadmap of what to expect.

Section I treats "Biblical Matters," and starts with Fr. Moloney's "Joy and Sorrow in the Infancy Stories." While some thinkers portray Matthew's and Luke's infancy narratives as conflicting with each other, Fr. Moloney sees them as complementary: Matthew's treatment features the painful sorrows surrounding Jesus' birth (such as the slaughter of the innocents) while Luke emphasizes the joy (such as the Magnificat). In Chapter 2, Fr. Mark Latcovich guides the reader through the rich tapestry of Scriptural texts that are proclaimed at Christmas. In Chapter 3, Fr. Larry Tosco, CSJ, takes up the significance of the Old Testament for Christian thinkers. Even if it is read anew in the light of Christ, might the Church also benefit from the possible reading that may be given it in strictly Jewish terms? In Chapter 4, Fr. Tosco challenges his readers to think more deeply about whether it is meaningful to claim that Jesus founded the Church. After all, the People of God had existed for centuries by the time Jesus was born; nevertheless, the Church would be impossible without Jesus. In Chapter 5, Fr. Tosco takes up the fundamentalist notion of the Book of Revelation, especially as it has been portrayed in the popular *Left Behind* series of novels, and exposes three common myths about Revelation. Finally, in Chapter 6, Fr. Mark Ott delves into the Book of Acts to find clues on how to evangelize so that the "new evangelization" might benefit from the experience of the first evangelization in the early church.

Section II deals with "The Splendor of the Human." Dr. Chad Engelland leads with a philosophical discussion in Chapter 7 entitled, "How Different Are We from Dogs, Chimps, and Dolphins?" He supports his case by noting how the local Museum of Natural History, apparently sensing the special difference that humans make, unwittingly puts human beings in a category separate from nature—and rightly so. In Chapter 8, Dr. Engelland further explores the difference between humans and animals by considering why human reproduction is so different from the breeding of animals. In Chapter 9, Dr. Engelland takes on today's most famous atheist, Richard Dawkins, and explains why his scientific methods and theories simply cannot cope with questions about God. In Chapter 10, Fr. Damian Ference treats philosophically a comment that is commonly heard even about people who commit crimes: "Deep down he was a good man." Was he? Fr. Ference shows that distinctions between being and behavior can make sense of such comments. In Chapter 11, Fr. Mike Woost challenges the reader to, "Say 'Amen' to who you are!" One way to view the "Splendor of the Human" is to consider along with St. Augustine that each person receiving communion is in the Body of Christ. Finally, Fr. Woost extends those reflections in Chapter 12 where he relates his experiences ministering with Bl. Mother Teresa's Missionaries of Charity who were called to be "tabernacles of flesh and blood."

Section III features articles that dwell on what can be called "The Summertime of the Soul" because the chapters treat issues associated with the relaxation that summertime typically brings. In Chapter 13, Sr. Mary McCormick, OSU, advises that as people slow down during summer, they ought to take the opportunity to contemplate and appreciate God's grace in leisure. She gives several practical suggestions about how this might be done. In Chapter 14, Fr. Mark Latcovich urges readers to take more seriously the Sabbath rest as a way to rejuvenate the soul. In Chapter 15, Fr. Damian Ference turns to Thomas Aquinas for surprising advice for those who become dragged down with the summertime blues. Finally, in Chapter 16, Sr. Mary McCormick calls readers to be attentive to the fact that faith is not only a "what" that is passed on, but also "a means by which" those realities are passed on. Faith pertains both to content and process.

Section IV deals with spirituality. In Chapter 17, Dr. Ed Kaczuk reflects on the conviction that, for a Christian, there really are no coincidences. Drawing on personal experience as well as on Saint John Paul II, he considers coincidence as occurring only within the designs of providence. Fr. John Loya looks at spirituality in a very practical way in Chapter 18. Applying an insight from spiritual master Anthony de Mello, SJ, he poses three simple questions to enable the reader to discern whether a message is coming from God or whether it is merely emanating from the dominant culture. For any reader who has ever cheated on a diet, Fr. Loya might provide some help in Chapter 19 where he distinguishes between physical hunger and spiritual hunger (which can never be satisfied through one more dessert). In Chapter 20, Fr. Loya urges readers not to let their emotions get the better of them. He poses five questions that might suggest ways for readers to regain control. In Chapter 21, Fr. Mark Latcovich calls attention to the famous 15th century Russian icon by Andrei Rublev to lead readers in a spiritual reflection on the Trinity. Finally, in Chapter 22, Fr. Mark Hollis provides a sampling of some of the new saints that appear in the latest edition of the Roman Missal.

Section V takes up matters of the liturgical life. In Chapter 23, Fr. Damian Ference sees great meaning in the new translation of the dismissal at Mass, "Go in peace, glorifying the Lord by your life." The Eucharist does not end in the church building, but must find its way into every corner of the world. In Chapter 24, Dr. Kaczuk illustrates the power of symbol by reporting on his personal experience of the Vietnam Veterans' Memorial in Washington, D.C. The Memorial made him look at that war in a new way, a way that could bring healing to a very difficult chapter in U.S. history. In Chapter 25, "Why Is Mass So Boring," I analyze an all too common experience at Mass. The liturgy does not resemble a pep rally prior to a college football game as much as it resembles a cooling-off period, a time-out, that tries to get us to calm down. Such liturgical experiences can frustrate the restless. In Chapter 26, Fr. Andy Turner coaxes readers to reflect on how they judge whether Lenten penances are successful or not. Rather than counting the additional prayers or times of fasting, he suggests that concentrating on the fruitfulness of Lent might be more helpful. In Chapter 27, Fr. Mike Woost reflects on a poem by St. Thérèse of Lisieux. He takes seriously the profound implications of her claim that, "I am a living Monstrance." In Chapter 28, I follow up that reflection with the opposite experience when a person is denied the Eucharist in certain circumstances. Although the Church never finally shuts the door on anyone, at times it must use the denial of communion to call attention to serious matters that must be addressed. Finally in Chapter 29, Fr. Mark Hollis offers a meditation on how the love of married couples reflect the love of Christ for his Bride, the Church.

Section VI delves into life and death issues, and certain moral quandaries and dilemmas that face Catholics today. In Chapter 30, I raise the recent problems surrounding military leaders who try to curb sexual abuse among the troops. While the military must cultivate a culture of death to become proficient in war, it will necessarily struggle to avoid the sins that cultures of death typically bring. In Chapter 31, Fr. Mark Ott calls attention to the media's misuse of the term "celibacy" to mean any period when one refrains from sexual relations. This results in the term "chastity" no longer having a place in today's secularized culture. In Chapter 32, Fr. Joe Koopman presents the views of the Church on stem cell research. While the Church has explicitly opposed the destruction of embryonic life as a source for stem cells, it actually encourages research using adult stem cells. In Chapter 33, Fr. Koopman explains the very nuanced treatment that the Church brings to end-of-life issues. The Church supports neither the position that biological life must be sustained at all costs, nor the position that a person's life depends only on one's usefulness to society. In Chapter 34, Fr. Koopman presents the Church's teaching on cremation. Not all practices can be condoned, but only those that express proper respect for the body, and an affirmation of the doctrine of the resurrection of the body. Finally, in Chapter 35, Sr. Mary McCormick explains the Christian sense of praying for the dead. Rooted in a firm belief in the union of the church on earth with the communion of saints in heaven, her reflections enhance our understanding of the Church's commemoration of the dead, especially in November when we call the deceased to mind in a special way.

Finally in Section VII, reflections turn to a consideration of God's call in people's lives. Especially teenagers and young adults need to discern God's call carefully since important decisions loom on the near horizon. In Chapter 36, Fr. Andy Turner describes an annual festival held on the grounds of the seminaries each year. The FEST mimics World Youth Day, and gathers families in a way that coaxes youngsters and teens to consider God's call through music, prayer, games and casual talks with clergy and religious. In Chapter 37, Fr. Mike McCandless, the Diocesan Vocation Director, reflects on the power of personal invitation to encourage young men to consider priesthood and women to consider religious life. In Chapter 38, Fr. McCandless offers lyrics by composer and musician Matt Maher to help readers to consider our youngsters as a Garden of Eden that Jesus is trying to cultivate. He views the FEST as a perfect opportunity to assist the Lord in this work. Finally, in Chapter 39, Dr. Ed Kaczuk offers his thoughts on the formation process that has led so many young men to ordination in the Diocese. He wisely remarks that while formation begins in the seminary, it continues throughout the priesthood. Finally in Chapter 40, Fr. Mark Hollis describes certain benchmarks of priestly identity that might prove helpful for those discerning a call to the priesthood.

For the reader's convenience, at the end of the book an alphabetical listing of authors appears together with their academic credentials. One final note, references to the Catechism of the Catholic Church are designated as "*CCC*" followed by the paragraph number. The numbers following Thomas Aquinas' *Summa Theologica* ("*ST*") refer to the Part, Question, and Article where the material may be found. Authors refer to Biblical books by standard abbreviations.

Let me take this opportunity thank the President-Rector, Fr. Mark Latcovich, for his wonderful leadership in bringing the two seminaries together closer than ever before. His kindness and continued encouragement of seminarians, students, faculty and staff are greatly appreciated by all.

On behalf of both seminary faculties, I sincerely hope that these chapters will be useful in advancing the faith of those who read them. May the grace of St. Mary Seminary and Borromeo Seminary prove to be a continued blessing for the people of the Diocese of Cleveland.

Rev. Gerald J. Bednar, Ph.D.
Vice-President/Vice-Rector
St. Mary Seminary and Graduate School of Theology

Section I

Biblical Matters

Chapter 1

JOY AND SORROW
IN THE INFANCY STORIES

by Rev. Francis J. Moloney, SDB

Institute for Religion and Critical Inquiry
Australian Catholic University,
Melbourne, Victoria, Australia, and
2013 Mullen Scholar in Residence at
Cleveland St. Mary Seminary

The Christmas pageantry that plays such an important role in the period surrounding the celebration of the Birth of Jesus on December 25th each year is full of joy. There is only one moment when something more sombre breaks into the celebration: the Feast of the Holy Innocents (December 28th). An atmosphere of joy is generated by the fact that the Churches use the Infancy Story of the Gospel of Luke (Lk. 1:1-2:52) as the inspiration for its Christmas pageantry. Indeed, in the Catholic tradition, what we call "the Joyful Mysteries" of the Rosary provide a summary of the Lukan message: Annunciation (Lk. 1:26-38), the Visitation (1:39-56), the Birth of Our Lord (2:1-21), the Presentation of Jesus in the Temple (2:22-38), and the Finding of the Child Jesus in the Temple (2:41-52).

The role of John the Baptist, so important for Luke that he is also announced (to Zechariah: 1:5-25), and his birth and naming is described (1:57-80), does not appear at Christmas. As both John the Baptist and his cousin Jesus are presented side-by side across the Lukan story, there is the record of the encounter between the two mothers (the Visitation: 1:39-56), so that Elizabeth can sing the praises of Mary, and recognise the forthcoming birth of Jesus. No matter how wonderful the conception, birth, and naming of John the Baptist, Jesus is more wonderful, for he "will be called holy, the Son of God" (1:35).

There should be no doubt in the mind of the reader or the listener that Jesus is far more important than John, great indeed as he was. Elizabeth's words to Mary, and Mary's rendering glory to God in the *Magnificat* make that clear. As Christmas-time is the celebration of Jesus, the equally joyful and wonderful conception, birth and naming of John the Baptist does not play a major role, although his person and message are very important through the Gospel readings of the Advent Season.

In the midst of such joy, where does the story of the slaying of all the innocent young males at Bethlehem, whose "martyrdom" is celebrated on December 28, come from? The answer, of course, is that it forms an important element in the Infancy Story of the Gospel of Matthew (1:1-2:23). It is closely associated with the role of the three Wise Men from the East, who do play a cameo role at Christmas-time, especially in the many Cribs that are constructed all over the world. Indeed, they are especially celebrated on January 6, the Feast of the Epiphany; they represent the coming of the whole world to worship the new-born King (see Mt. 2:2, 11). In many places only the Lukan shepherds (Lk. 2:8-14) are placed in the Crib for December 25, and the Matthean Wise Men join the Lukan shepherds later—on January 6th.

While these Wise Men have been taken from the Gospel of Matthew in order to add to the joy of the Christmas pageantry, they in fact play a more sombre role in Matthew 1-2. Seeking a King whose star they have divined in the heavens, they introduce consternation, anger and violence (Mt. 2:3, 7-8, 16-18). Warned in a dream, they must return home via a different route, in order to avoid the wicked King Herod (Mt. 2:12). No commentator on the experiences of the Wise Men has quite captured their ambiguous role quite as poignantly as T. S. Eliot in his *The Journey of the Magi*. No doubt they indicate, from the beginnings of Matthew's story, that Jesus' mission will reach out to the ends of the earth (28:16-20), but at what cost?

If we were to construct Mysteries of the Rosary from Matthew 1-2, they would stand side by side with our current Sorrowful Mysteries: a genealogy (1:1-17), the news of an illegitimate conception in which execution must be avoided by the good St. Joseph (1:18-25), the danger of two Kings in Israel: Herod and Jesus (2:1-12), the slaying of the innocents (2:16-18), necessitating the flight (2:13-15) and the eventual return from Egypt (2:19-23), only to find that a further wicked King is on the throne. This leads to a further flight: to Nazareth (2:22-23). There is very little obvious "joy" in these episodes, and behind them lies a great deal of misunderstanding, death, pain and "sorrow."

Much ink has been spilt over the two Infancy Stories in the Gospels, especially in attempts to show that while they seem to tell different stories, they can be harmonized. Until recent times, the most heard explanation for the differences has been that the Gospel of Luke tells the story from Mary's perspective, but the

Gospel of Matthew reports Joseph's perspective. But this will not do! As one commentator once wrote: if that is true, then one wonders what level and quality of communication took place between Mary and Joseph. They must have had very little in common if they recalled these events so differently, even to the point of not agreeing upon whether they began their lives together in Nazareth (Lk. 1:26-27) or Bethlehem (Mt. 1:18-2:12). That is normally something that couples remember.

Admittedly, and importantly, there are many shared elements in the two stories: Herod, Joseph, Mary, virginal conception, Bethlehem, Nazareth, the name Jesus, and many other details. There is something "back there" in the tradition that joins these stories, but we simply do not have sufficient evidence to reconstruct any such source. But that should not concern us. In the end, these wonderful stories proclaim what God has done for us in and through Jesus. The Infancy Stories of Luke and Matthew are not to be *contrasted*, but read and meditated *side-by-side*, so that they might complement one another and thus enrich our Christian tradition and nourish Christian spirituality.

If that is the case, why is there so much "sorrow" in Matthew 1-2? The author of the Gospel of Matthew has sometimes been called "meticulous Matthew." He is extremely careful in the composition of his story, and one of his concerns is to show, from the very beginnings of the life of Jesus, that this man will be surrounded by conflict, death and difficulty. Indeed, many of the words that appear in the Infancy Narrative about the consternation of Herod and the people when the Wise Men ask about the birth of the new-born King are repeated when Matthew tells of a similar consternation among the people and their leaders at Jesus' trial and execution. But is it all "sorrow"? Blended splendidly into Matthew's story of Jesus' origins (1:1-17), conception (1:18-25), birth (2:1-12), and subsequent experiences (2:13-23) is the indication that the coming of Jesus, for all the difficulties that it may produce for those who commit themselves to him (Joseph, Mary, the Wise Men), is the long-awaited fulfilment of God's promises to Israel: "this was to fulfil" (see 1:22-23; 2:5-6, 15, 17-18, 23).

It is common Christian experience that the ways of God, indicated to us in and through the fulfilment of Sacred Scripture, are often not the ways of our contemporary society and culture. Crucial, in this respect, is the promise of the Word of God that opens the Gospel of Matthew, and the Word of Jesus that closes it. Despite the conflict that can emerge from a courageous Christian presence in today's secular society, the birth of Jesus fulfils the promise of Isaiah: "'Behold a virgin shall conceive and bear a son, and his name shall be Emmanuel' (which means God with us)" (1:23). His final words in the Gospel of Matthew indicate that this promise shall not be thwarted: "I am with you always, to the close of the age" (28:20).

Although Matthew highlights the darkness and Luke the light, the *contrasting* Infancy Accounts of the Gospels of Luke and Matthew proclaim the *same* message: the never failing presence of the love of God whose Son came "to give light to those who sit in darkness and in the shadow of death, to guide our feet into the way of peace" (Lk. 1:78-79).

Chapter 2

Christmas Everyday

By Mark A. Latcovich

"One of the most important elements in the spiritual life is the ability to come alive and see the splendor, value and beauty in ordinary things," writes Trappist monk Thomas Merton. Our celebration of Christmas affords us an opportunity to gaze into the beauty of this season's rich spirituality as discovered in the scriptural texts of the Church's Christmas liturgies. The readings for Christmas at the *vigil mass*, *mass at midnight*, *mass at dawn* and *mass during the day* create a tapestry of images and themes as God's plan for salvation unfolds.

The *vigil Mass* (Is. 62:1-5) begins with the image of a royal marriage between God and Israel. Here the once forsaken Israel, who wandered forty years in the desert, fought for possession of her land, only to have it destroyed while she remained in captivity, is called "spouse" by a God who delights in her and who promises to give her a new name. Many of the early Church Fathers read this text to prefigure the new Israel, the Church, born out of the Father's heart, and called by Jesus to be his beloved spouse. The second reading from the Acts of the Apostles (13:16-17, 22-25) describes how God alone has exalted his chosen people from the time of the Exodus to the ministry of John the Baptist pointing to the savior brought to Israel through King David's lineage.

Israel's promised redeemer will be its King. This is illustrated in the genealogy of Jesus from Matthew's Gospel (1:1-25). The Gospel highlights a lineage that shows Jesus to be a descendant of David tracing his lineage up to Joseph, while beginning his ancestry from Abraham the model of Israel's faith. Joseph's faith and actions are highlighted by his trust in the angel's words to him in a dream to take Mary as his wife and give her child the name Jesus (God-with-us).

All three of these readings illustrate how God works through the ordinary events of our day. We may not always see how our decisions, choices and actions are ultimately part of God's plan, but each day our faith and trust in God lead us into a blessed future.

Mass at midnight begins with the prophet Isaiah (9:1-6). The prophecies about the Messiah on David's throne tell us that unimaginable peace and perfect covenantal righteousness have finally dawned "now and forever." Jesus is the "God-hero" and "Prince of Peace" and is the one who exceeds all the powers and abilities of earthly leaders. Jesus brings light amid darkness and gloom, releasing people from their burdens and slavery. Paul's letter to Titus (2:11-14) views this light as the saving grace of God and expands the Messiah's reign to include "all people." The appearance of the glory of God is seen in Jesus "who gave himself for us" on the cross to "cleanse for himself a people as his own." The Gospel (Lk. 2:1-14) places Jesus' birth in Bethlehem, the city of David. A decree by Caesar Augustus brought Joseph and Mary to an overcrowded city that led to Mary, ". . . laying her child in a manger because there was no room for them in the inn." Luke creates wonderful irony in his account. Heavenly splendor spreads itself above the brutal poverty of stable and manger. Angelic voices announce a child whose dominion is vast, but tonight, he is seen only by a few shepherds.

These readings remind us that life's plans do not always go the way we imagine. Nevertheless, God is with us in difficult and challenging times and present with us even when it seems like divine help is far from where we find ourselves.

Mass at Dawn builds on the readings from the vigil and midnight using the same biblical books. Isaiah (62:11-12) completes the first reading from the vigil by naming Israel (and the Church) "his holy and redeemed people." The people are called "Frequented" because God's grace and mercy has filled their lives through this new and intimate relationship. Paul's letter to Titus (3:4-7) speaks of us as "heirs in hope of eternal life" because we have been justified through the grace of Christ and "the bath of rebirth and renewal by the Holy Spirit." God's kind and generous love is pure gift, and never merited by our own deeds. Luke's Gospel (2:15-20) takes us with the shepherds to the manger in Bethlehem. And like the shepherds, through our witness, we are to make known this child to others! Luke has Mary "reflecting" on these events in her heart.

These texts suggest that we need to pay attention to the events that unfold in our lives so as to yield a strong faith to keep us always prepared for the unexpected. Do we treasure these gifts of mercy and grace given to us through Christ and the sacraments of the Church enough to want to share them with others?

Mass during the day opens again with Isaiah (52:7-10) using the image of a messenger, "who brings glad tidings, announcing peace, bearing good news and salvation." This "messenger" has been the prophets, the angels and even the shepherds announcing God's plan of salvation in Christ to the "ends of the earth." The book of Hebrews (Heb. 1:1-6) summarizes how this plan of salvation is fulfilled in Jesus, who now sits at the right hand of the Father with angels worshiping him. The gospel is taken from John (1:1-18) where the Jesus is presented as the Word and Light of God to our world. The Word became human and lived among us to reveal the fullness of grace and truth.

These readings give us a portrait of how God's arrival in history is not a mere past event. God's arrival is taking place continually in the here and now. We have been showered with abundant gifts through Christ that are given again in every proclamation of the Word and Eucharistic liturgy. The splendor of Christmas is never a day, but a life-long journey God has invited us to embrace.

Chapter 3

IS THE OLD TESTAMENT FULFILLED BY CHRIST?

by Rev. Lawrence Tosco, CSJ

Around 150 A.D. Marcion, the wealthy and brilliant son of a bishop from Asia Minor, came to Rome proclaiming that Christians should do away with the Old Testament. Apparently, he wanted to move beyond the heated discussions with the synagogue about the right interpretation of the OT and push aside a book that seemed primitive and difficult to reconcile with Jesus' message of mercy and love.

While finding much popular support, Marcion met strong opposition by church leaders and scholars. Eventually, these won and saved the Old Testament for the church.

How did Marcion's opponents achieve this? By reading the Old Testament from the perspective of new events and beliefs, a practice already found within the Old Testament itself and the writings of the early followers of Jesus soon to be known as the New Testament. For these Christians, the events connected with Jesus and the church became the lens from which to re-read and understand the Old Testament. As a consequence, the Old Testament became announcement, sign, figure, "type," and "shadow" of the events surrounding the coming of Christ and the emergence of the church. In the process, the Old Testament became a Christian book.

As we look back today, we find their goal good and noble, but their approach rather imperfect. In fact, it is naïve to consider the Old Testament, especially the prophets, totally focused on the future, foretelling events fulfilled in Christ and the church. Today, thanks to the work of historical criticism, we have become aware of the fact that Christian interpretation of the Old Testament is shaped by our faith in Christ. The 2001 book-length document of the Pontifical Biblical Commission ("PBC"), *The Jewish People and Their Sacred Scriptures in the Christian Bible*, states that Christian reading of the Old Testament is "a retrospective perception whose point of departure is not in the text as such, but in the events of the New Testament proclaimed by apostolic preaching" (§ 21). It is these events, understood with the faith of the church, that lead us to read the Old Testament as announcement of the New. Without previous Christian faith such reading is arbitrary.

The naïve approach to the Old Testament had a cost, a grave one indeed. It tended to deny intrinsic value to the Old Testament as well as legitimacy to non-Christian readings. Often, this tendency was accompanied by a view that has become known as "supercessionism,"—for God, Judaism is finished, displaced by Christianity—with its bloody train of persecution and forced conversion. Let me explain. If the Old Testament is announcement and foreshadowing of Christian events, then it dissipates when the announced comes to pass, when the light dispels the shadow. If Christ is the only key to the Old Testament, then any other reading is illegitimate and wrong. And, if that is the case, then Judaism is a relic of the past, whose disappearance ought to be accelerated.

Things began to change with Vatican II. More recently, with John Paul II, we have come to understand that God's covenant with Israel is irrevocable. And the PBC document cited above adds: "Christians can and ought to admit that the Jewish reading of the Bible is a possible one, in continuity with the Jewish Sacred Scriptures from the Second Temple period, a reading analogous to the Christian reading which developed in parallel fashion" (§ 22).

Yet, the journey is not finished. When will all Christians overcome old prejudices about Judaism and the Old Testament? When will the long shadow of Marcion dissipate? And when will even good church documents, such as that of PBC, avoid the ambiguous and misleading language of "adumbration" or foreshadowing (§ 64), and display a real appreciation for the Old Testament in itself, for its role in the interpretation of the New, for its value as witness to the awesome mystery of God independently of New Testament fulfillment?

In an article evaluating strengths and weakness of the PBC document, written shortly before his recent death, Roland E. Murphy, a giant of American Catholic biblical scholarship, includes this quotation from Dietrich Bonhoeffer: "My thoughts and my feelings seem to be getting more and more like the Old Testament. . . . It is only when one knows the ineffability of the Name of God that one can utter the name of Jesus Christ. . . . I don't think it is

Christian to want to get to the New Testament too soon and too directly."[1]

Is the Old Testament fulfilled by Christ?

Yes, but . . . .

---

[1] Roland E. Murphy, "The Biblical Commission, the Jews, and Scriptures," *Biblical Theology Bulletin* 32, no. 3 (Summer, 2002): 147.

Chapter 4

Did Jesus Found the Church?

by Rev. Lawrence Tosco, CSJ

One of the most frustrating things in conversations about religion is the fact that some people want a "yes or no" answer to questions that have no such clear-cut answer. As a teacher of Scripture, I get these questions almost daily: Did Abraham exist? Did God give Moses the commandments? Did the prophets announce the coming of Jesus? Did Jesus know he was God? Did Jesus institute the priesthood? Does Revelation announce the end of the world?—all questions for which the best answer is probably "Yes, but . . ." or perhaps "No, but . . ." An explanation always needs to accompany either answer.

To those who hold onto clear and simple ideas, this may sound insufficient and confusing. But often it is the best we can do especially when it comes to questions that involve the interaction between God and humans. While necessary and valuable, in the end all our attempts are limited and insufficient. Who in fact can really pretend to grasp the mystery of God? Only fools or idolaters.

So, did Jesus found the Church? It all depends on what the question means.

No, Jesus did not found the Church, if by Church we mean the structured institution we have come to know over the centuries. He did not give his disciples a blueprint concerning governance, sacraments, and laws. To think that way is not only simplistic, but misguided. Think of it this way: Jesus could not have founded the Church because the Church had already existed for a long time—it was God's people, Israel, the "assembly of God." Jesus' ministry was not about the establishment of a separatist sect or a new religious community that would leave Judaism, "God's People," behind, and spread to the Gentile world. What the thoroughly Jewish Jesus, rooted in the prophetic tradition of his people, did was to call on his fellow Israelites in order to gather them into the community of the end time—a community renewed and restored through response to his message of God's mercy and acceptance of the last and the excluded. That's what he called the "Kingdom of God." There is no indication that Jesus foresaw a community separated from Israel, engaged in a mission to the Gentiles, becoming itself predominantly Gentile and developing the consciousness of being a different religion. This began to happen after Jesus' death and resurrection with the accompanying claims by his disciples that Jesus had been made Lord, had given them the Holy Spirit and sent them into mission first to Israel and then increasingly to the Gentiles.

And now to the "but . . . " part. The Church would not have been possible without the ministry of Jesus and the choices he had made. In other words, when understood as a process, the foundation of the Church goes back to Jesus. What in the ministry of Jesus provided the basis for the emergence of the Church? First and foremost, the circle of the Twelve which Jesus formed as a sign of the Israel he had been sent to gather. John Paul Meier notes that Jesus, ". . . chose to stand over against the circle of the Twelve as its founder instead of making himself one of its members."[2] He was their point of reference and their leader, the one to whom they pledged allegiance.

To them, and to a wider circle of disciples, he gave a number of things which, when taken together, provide an incipient organization. Among them is the practice of baptism, the mission to Israel, the stringent demands for discipleship, his special prayers and rules for community living. Add to these elements other distinguishing approaches to fasting, divorce, purity and Sabbath, sinners and marginalized, etc., and you have the foundation for the community that will develop after Easter. It will be a slow incremental process, influenced by memory and new situations, guided by the Spirit of Jesus active in his followers and the world. It is a process that continued for centuries and will never be completely done.

Rather sarcastically long ago someone said that while Jesus had announced the Kingdom what emerged was the Church. Yes, but . . . while it is not the Kingdom, the Church is undoubtedly its divinely willed, holy and sinful, instrument.

---

[2] John Paul Meier, *A Marginal Jew*, III: *Companions and Competitors*, (New York: Doubleday, 2001), 250.

Chapter 5

Revelation: Not What Some Think

by Fr. Lawrence Tosco, CSJ

Although the movie flopped, the *Left Behind* series,[3] which started appearing in the wake of the new millennium, did well. It may not be great literature, but many people found it interesting reading. And some have asked whether its story of rapture, tribulation, and judgment reflects a legitimate understanding of the book of Revelation and what God has in store for humanity.

Here I do not intend to review the *Left Behind* series, but with the new millennium safely underway, it is the right time to take another look at the Book of Revelation and some of the ways in which people approach it. For the sake of clarity and using the broad strokes unavoidable in such a brief treatment, I will challenge three common misunderstandings of the book of Revelation. Let's call them "myths."

---

[3] Tim LaHaye and Jerry Jenkins, *Left Behind: A Novel of the Earth's Last Days* (Colorado Springs, CO: Alive Publications, 1995) plus four other related novels.

Myth one: Revelation is all about things to come, about the end of the world. Not true: while not disinterested in the final fulfillment of the plan of God for creation, Revelation is not centered on future events, but on the world-transforming event that we celebrate at Easter. At the center of Revelation is the Lamb, "slain" but "standing" who, at Easter, has forever changed the world.

Revelation proclaims that for the followers of the Lamb, just as for him, there is victory in defeat, there is life in death, and there is hope for the faithful. By means of strategically placed heavenly scenes of praise and celebration, Revelation offers the divine perspective on reality, how things really are. In Ch. 7, for instance, those who have survived the trial (by dying!) are dressed in white robes (made white in the blood of the Lamb!) and hold palm branches (they are victors!). For the original readers, and for readers of all times, the message is the same and clear: in Christ, your witness, your self-giving love and, when necessary, even the sacrifice of your life, whether literal or daily, joins you with the victorious crowd before the throne.

No matter how things may appear here on earth, in heaven (in reality!) you are victorious—a victory that is celebrated and made present in the liturgical assembly, a real slice of heaven where time and space are collapsed. Revelation has nothing to say about the end of the world, except the assurance that this creation has an "end," i.e., a direction and goal, namely the communion of God with humanity symbolized by the marriage of the Lamb and the City-Bride (Rev. 21:2).

Myth two: Revelation announces divine judgment on evildoers. Not true: Revelation's central message is not judgment, but salvation. The protagonists of the Book of Revelation are the followers of the Lamb, the struggling and persecuted disciples. It is their salvation that Revelation is all about. The others, the oppressors, the idolaters, the followers of the beast, the unbelievers are only a foil for the divine operation of rescuing his own.

Many details in the cyclic story of Revelation remind the attentive reader of the story of Exodus, including a whole section (Ch. 15-16) that is patterned on the plagues of Egypt. Like Exodus, so too Revelation describes God's powerful intervention to save his own. Indeed Exodus' concern is not the destruction of the Egyptians, but the liberation of Israel. The destruction of the Egyptians is nothing more than "collateral damage" to the divine rescue operation. A rabbinic story relates that while the Egyptians were drowning in the sea, the angels started clapping and cheering. But God silenced them saying, "Aren't the Egyptian my people, too?" In truth, God wants all to be saved.

Such is also the wonderful outlook of Revelation. When, in the imaginative poetry of the conclusion, the symbols of oppression and unbelief, the harlot-city, the beast, the nations and their kings, have been destroyed and the faithful City, the City-Bride, comes down from heaven, we are told that its gates are always open, the nations are welcome, and there is a medicinal tree for their healing. Truly, God's only business is that of salvation.

Myth three: Revelation glorifies war and violence. Not true: while Revelation does use the old symbol known as "holy war," a symbol that dominates the story of the Exodus and the conquest of the Promised Land, it dramatically subverts it. When in Ch. 19, at the height of the divine "rescue operation," Jesus the King of kings and Lord of lords, appears on a white horse, we are told that his cloak has been dipped in blood. Before the battle starts, he is already bloody, with his own blood. Not only that, but his weapon is described as the "sword of his mouth," his word, his witness, his faithful witness (martyrdom!) before Pilate, and the witness of his followers, the giving of his life which truly rescues and changes the world.

So we come full circle: Revelation proclaims the victory of God at Easter, a victory that spans the ages and forever changes the world, a victory we celebrate around the table of the Lord and in daily witness of love, ". . . as we await the blessed hope and the coming of our Savior Jesus Christ."[4]

---

[4]*Roman Missal*, third edition, trans. International Commission on English in the Liturgy Corp., (New Jersey: Catholic Book Publishing Corp., 2011), 517.

Chapter 6

What the First Evangelization Can Teach the New Evangelization

by Rev. Mark Ott

Just before Jesus ascended into heaven, he promised his followers that they would receive the Holy Spirit, who would empower them to be his witnesses "in Jerusalem, throughout Judea and Samaria, and to the ends of the earth" (Acts 1:8). The story of the Acts of the Apostles then unfolds exactly as he said it would. After receiving the Spirit at Pentecost (ch. 2), these first Christians proclaim and imitate the words and deeds of Jesus, first in Jerusalem (2:14-8:1), then in Judea and Samaria (8:2-9:43), and then to more distant cities via missionary journeys (10:1-28:31).

This inspired evangelical activity has continued up to today, with the result that about one third of the world's 7 billion people now identify themselves as Christian, with about half of the world's Christians being Roman Catholic. The task today for this large Church is to make sure that all who identify themselves as Christian actually live this out in a vibrant and meaningful way. This is really the driving force behind the New Evangelization that is now being eagerly promoted throughout the Church. But just because this evangelization is "new," that doesn't mean we need to reinvent the wheel to make it happen. There is plenty we can learn from the "first evangelization" to help us in the New Evangelization.

The first lesson the early Christians teach us is that an evangelizer is someone who above all *knows Jesus*. When the apostles were seeking a replacement for Judas their main criterion for the job was that this new apostle, ". . . accompanied [them] the whole time the Lord Jesus came and went among [them]," and the primary job description was to ". . . become with [them] a witness to his resurrection" (1:21-22). Once they receive the Spirit and begin their evangelical work, the main content of their message revolved around *who Jesus is* and *how they had experienced him*. We see this in the great speeches they deliver (cf. 2:14-36; 3:12-26; 7:1-53, etc.), their testimony under trial, (cf. 5:27-32), and as the context and power by which they are able to heal and do other amazing things (cf. 9:32-43).

Obviously, we did not witness the earthly ministry of Jesus the way the original apostles did. But the core of our evangelical message should be the same as theirs. We need to be ready to witness to people, whenever the opportunity arises, about *who Jesus is* for us, and *how we have experienced him*. How have you experienced the risen Jesus in your life? Consider, for example, how you have encountered him in the liturgy, in personal prayer, though the ministry and witness of others, or walking with you during a significant life experience. The more vividly you can recollect these ideas *for yourself*, the easier it will be for you to witness them *to others*.

A second lesson early Christians lesson is that an evangelizer relies on prayer for guidance and inspiration.

Even before Pentecost, Jesus' followers were already forming their community in the context of prayer (cf. 1:14). This continues and expands as their evangelical ministry takes off. They pray when they need to make decisions (cf. 1:24), for ongoing community formation (cf. 2:42), as they start to encounter resistance (cf. 4:23-31), when they travel (cf. 21:5-6) or just as an integral part of their daily routine (cf. 10:9). Prayer is not something "extra" that they do; it is a natural and nourishing element of every facet of their lives.

Modern Christians often confess, "I should probably pray more than I do," but then seldom take the next step of discerning what this means. Take the time to prayerfully evaluate your prayer life. Given your state in life, when and how should you be praying? Mornings and/or evenings? Before big decisions at work or at home? As you are putting the kids on the school bus? Before you go out on a date? And what should be the content of your prayer times? Actively discerning the role of prayer in your life can really help to increase its effectiveness for you.

A third lesson we can learn is that an evangelizer is courageous because of the fortitude that comes from the Holy Spirit. The early Christians kept on preaching, in spite of trial (4:1-22), persecution (8:1-3), storms and shipwrecks (27:6-44), seemingly ineffective preaching (cf. 17:32), and even martyrdom (7:54-60). This courage, however, was not rooted in their own self-confidence, but in their absolute certainty that the Holy Spirit was guiding their ways. We may not face the same difficulties as they, but still need courage to embrace the often counter-cultural ideals that are integral to our faith.

Ultimately, these three points are deeply related. The better I understand who Jesus is and how he acts in my life, the more I will want to deepen that relationship through prayerful communication with him. And the richer my prayer life, the more confident I will be in the Holy Spirit's guidance. This, then, is a great recipe for a successful New Evangelization: allow the Lord to really touch and transform your life, and then witness to others about the joy and hope that comes from his love and mercy.

Section II

The Splendor of the Human

Chapter 7

How Different Are We from Dogs, Chimps, and Dolphins?

by Dr. Chad Engelland

According to the narrative of *Genesis*, we are made out of dust. The text clearly teaches the lowly origins of the human race. Thus, it should be no cause of scandal to believers that science has uncovered convincing evidence that we are biologically related to chimpanzees and other living beings. As the earth brought forth plants, crawling things, and wild animals, so it paved the way for us.

Of course, *Genesis* also teaches that we humans, alone among God's earthly creatures, are made in the image and likeness of God. We alone are geared toward eternal life. Should we Christians be embarrassed by this claim to uniqueness? After all, today we know that the human genome is 96 percent similar to a chimpanzee genome. How big of a difference could 4 percent make?

At the Cleveland Museum of Natural History, the first exhibit humorously depicts a snake, a monkey, and an ostrich sitting in front of a TV. What show are they watching? Via a surveillance camera, they are watching you, the visitor to the museum. The exhibit cleverly highlights human uniqueness: humans watch the nature channel, but nature does not watch the human channel.

What gives us this perch above the world so that we can do science and contemplate nature? Language and understanding are the keys to this human capability.

Other animals are interested in eating and reproducing, but humans are also interested in understanding. We want to do biologically irrelevant things like maintain zoos, study tigers, paint tigers, and pretend that a stuffed piece of fabric is a tiger.

Even the youngest children, studies show, differ from chimpanzees in the use of gestures.[5] Children want to share the world and thus happily point out biologically irrelevant things: Airplane! By contrast, chimpanzees use gestures to motivate their trainer to give them something to eat: Gimme banana! When children grow up they continue to do biologically useless things like build the international space station and the Rock and Roll Hall of Fame. Chimps continue to focus on eating.

Darwin wanted to blur the difference between humans and other animals. However, even he admitted that language opens up self-understanding: "It may be freely admitted that no animal is self-conscious, if by this term it is implied, that he reflects on such points, as whence he comes or whither he will go, or what is life and death, and so forth."[6]

---

[5] See Michael Tomasello, *Why We Cooperate* (Cambridge, MA: The MIT Press, 2009).
[6] Charles Darwin, *The Descent of Man* in Darwin, *Great Books of the Western World*, Vol. 49 (Chicago: Encyclopedia Britannica, 1952), 297.

Because we humans can understand, we have free will and moral responsibility. Consider Bethany Hamilton, an inspiring teenage surfer whose arm was bitten off by a shark. She should not hold it against the shark, because it was just being a shark. But imagine if a human being had mauled off her arm. She would be right to hold him responsible (she should forgive him, no doubt, but you can only forgive someone who is responsible for what he did — it would make no sense for Bethany to forgive the shark). Humans can understand what is right, and therefore they are morally responsible.

Because we humans are morally responsible, we are made for a specific kind of communion. Sure otters and ants, dogs and dolphins, likewise commune with one another. Humans, however, contribute to a common good that we all knowingly and responsibly participate in. We therefore can form marriages and political institutions. There could be no political freedoms for dogs, chimps, and dolphins, but there are human freedoms that no political power can morally violate.

At the Cleveland Museum of Natural History, an exhibit on the negative impact humans make on the environment says, "Changes in climate are usually natural ones. Not this time." What does it mean to say that changes we cause aren't natural? Aren't we part of nature, too? The idea seems to be this: Because we humans can figure out how nature works and because we are responsible for what we do, we are not just part of nature. We're also stewards of nature.

In this way, philosophy can confirm what *Genesis* teaches. Humans are different from other animals, because humans alone can understand and speak about nature (2:19), exercise moral responsibility (3:11), live in light of a common good (2:23), and have dominion over the earth (1:26). These differences mean we are the only animals that can hear God and speak to him, the only ones that can love God and neighbor, and the only ones that can share in the work of his providence.

Biologically, we're only 4 percent different than some other animals. But philosophically, we're separated from all other animals by a great difference. To explain the difference, the Church sensibly maintains that God gives to each human being a spiritual soul, which takes up and transfigures the meaning of our biological inheritance.

Chapter 8

Why Having Children Is Deeply Meaningful and Beautiful

by Dr. Chad Engelland

O f the philosopher Elizabeth Anscombe, the following story is told. Having just had her seventh child, she returned to her Oxford classroom to find that someone had scrawled on the blackboard the insult: "Anscombe breeds." She responded by adding two words to the board: "immortal beings." Elizabeth, you see, was intentionally doing something quite different from animal breeding. With her husband, the philosopher Peter Geach, she was bringing into existence immortal beings.

In August of 2013, *Time Magazine* ran a cover story on the increasing number of married couples who deliberately choose not to have children. The cover shows a husband and wife lounging on the beach with the headline: "The Childfree Life: When Having It All Means Not Having Children." The same week, a well-publicized study found that women with higher IQs have a decreased desire to reproduce.

Elizabeth Anscombe and Peter Geach are two of the twentieth century's most influential philosophers. They deliberately chose to have children, because they

32

understood that it is not a matter of perpetuating the species or passing on genes but something else entirely. Following the lead of these two Catholic philosophers, we can distinguish between the biological act, *reproduction*, and the personal act, *procreation*.

(1) Animals reproduce. They don't seek offspring. After all, they don't know anything about "the birds and the bees." They just do what they feel the urge to do. Sometimes there is a powerful emotional bonding, as with the Reed Titi Monkeys, and sometimes there isn't, as with Sand Sharks. Animals seek release, pleasure, and sometimes emotional fulfillment, and unbeknownst to them, Mother Nature uses those desires to perpetuate the species (or re-produce).

(2) We humans, by contrast, can do something quite different: procreate. We not only have the inclination for pleasure and a desire for emotional bonding, but also *intelligence* to know the basics of the birds and bees. We know what naturally results when we fulfill our inclinations and yield to our desires. We humans also have *freedom*. Understanding what sex is, we can engage in it willfully or decide not to do so.

Because we have intelligence and freedom, we are *persons*, not just animals. When a human being comes to be, we're not dealing with just another member of the biological species, *homo sapiens*. We're dealing with a being that can never be produced again: a particular person.

The human being, knowing what sex is about, can freely engage in it, precisely so that there might come to be another human person. In this way, human parents are not used by Mother Nature to perpetuate the species. Parents are co-participants in a basically personal process. They can knowingly and freely serve the noblest of ends: participation in the creation of another person.

Procreation comes into even sharper focus when there is awareness that our personal nature implies immortality. As beings with intelligence and freedom, we exceed our biology and are capable of existing beyond the grave. Reproduction seeks the immortality of the species, but procreation seeks the immortal person. Humans, themselves immortal, can engage in sex as persons: knowingly and willingly inviting the coming to be of another immortal human person.

The fact that another person comes to be implies the need for far greater discrimination regarding one's sexual partner than occurs elsewhere in nature. The child establishes new personal identities for the parents; with her advent the parents take on the role of "mother" or "father," and their relation to each other becomes further entwined for the rest of their lives as parent to each other's child.

It is principally in view of procreation as the natural result of sex, that those who would engage in it are morally obliged to first marry. "I take you to be the mother (or father) of my potential children." Marriage makes the difference between something that is merely *biological*, reproduction, and something that is *personal*, procreation.

Procreation doesn't end when a baby is born. Parents have to raise and educate the child they've brought into existence. Their concern should not be limited to making sure their children can get a good job when they grow up. Most importantly, parents must make sure their children understand what makes for a meaningful life, including those things that make life worth sharing with others. Parents — and not schools or popular culture — are the primary educators in what it means to be human.

Reflecting on the Year of Faith in 2013, Pope Francis invited people to rediscover the meaning and beauty of procreation: "Faith also helps us to grasp in all its depth and richness the begetting of children, as a sign of the love of the Creator who entrusts us with the mystery of a new person" (*On Faith*, n. 52).

Chapter 9

Science, Science Fiction, and Real Life

by Dr. Chad Engelland

B efore becoming the most influential atheist alive, Richard Dawkins was a popular science writer. In the international bestseller, *The Selfish Gene*, he argued that our genes engineered us for the sole purpose of reproducing them: "We are survival machines—robot vehicles blindly programmed to preserve the selfish molecules known as genes."[7] Or more ominously: "They are in you and in me; they created us, body and mind; and their preservation is the ultimate rationale for our existence."[8]

In a new edition of the book, Dawkins quotes a letter from a reader who wishes he could "unread" the book: "I largely blame *The Selfish Gene* for a series of bouts of depression I suffered from for more than a decade. . . Never sure of my spiritual outlook on life, but trying to

---

[7] Richard Dawkins, *The Selfish Gene* (Oxford: Oxford Univeristy Press, 2006), xxi.
[8] *Ibid.*, 20.

find something deeper—trying to believe, but not quite being able to—I found that this book just about blew away any vague ideas I had along these lines."[9]

Dawkins responds, "Presumably there is indeed no purpose in the ultimate fate of the cosmos, but do any of us really tie our life's hopes to the ultimate fate of the cosmos anyway? Of course we don't; not if we are sane."[10]

Dawkins's cavalier response reminds me of one of his favorite authors, Douglas Adams. In Adams's sci-fi classic, *Hitchhiker's Guide to the Galaxy*, people get together to build the world's biggest computer in order to ask it the most important question: what's the meaning of life, the universe, and everything? After grinding away on the problem for millions of years, the computer was ready with the answer. People gathered together with great anticipation. The answer, according to the computer, was "42."

What kind of answer should we expect a computer to give us? Of course, a computational machine will give us a computational answer. That is what computers do.

In a similar way, what kind of answer should we expect science to give us? The genius of modern scientific method is to consider only what can be quantified and mathematically modeled. That is why it has put us on the moon, engineered nuclear reactors, and outfitted us with GPS units.

Now, whatever the meaning of life might be, it is not something that can be quantified and modeled, and so

---

[9] *Ibid.*, xiii.
[10] *Ibid.*, xiii.

it is not something that modern science can answer. This is not a criticism of science, but simply a limitation of its method.

Dawkins admits that there is more to life than science: "Our lives are ruled by all sorts of closer, warmer, human ambitions and perceptions."[11]   Among these, Dawkins counts scientific wonder and poetry. The famous physicist Stephen Hawking says this about his children and grandchildren: "They have taught me that science is not enough. I need the warmth of family life."[12]   What is this warmth of which these scientists speak?

Perhaps telescopes, microscopes, and computer simulations keep us from seeing what is right before our naked eyes. Might the meaning of human life be love? Not love as a euphoric feeling, not love as pheromones or oxytocin, but love which *reveals to us the depths of reality*. The love that makes us spontaneously proclaim, "Lord, it is good for us to be here."

Love eludes science, but love cannot elude the scientist if he or she is to find life worth living.

Is such a love a cosmic accident? An unintended byproduct of mindless and loveless matter?   Is the presence of human freedom and love a cosmic anomaly or the reason for the cosmos?   Science cannot decide, but each of us, scientists and non-scientists alike, must decide. What evidence is there for us to go on?

---

[11] *Ibid.*, xiii.
[12] "Inside a Great Mind: The Parade Interview of Stephen Hawking," September 12, 2010 www.parade.com/37704/parade/12-inside-a-great-mind/. Accessed 1/16/2014.

The God who pronounces, "I am who am," and who nonetheless empties himself to die on a cross reveals that this cosmos, unfolding from the big bang forward, involving progressive evolution of life, has as its origin and end an infinite power that is infinite love. Science can aid us in our wonder before such powerful love, but it cannot explain it or manufacture it.

Incidentally, if you visit Google and ask "the answer to the ultimate question of life the universe and everything," it replies, predictably, "42."

Chapter 10

Is There Such a Thing as a Bad Person?

by Fr. Damian J. Ference

"Deep down he was a good man." "If you really knew her like I do, you would know that she has good heart." These are the sorts of things we hear after some man has killed his family or robbed a bank, or after a woman has beat her children or stolen jewelry from her elderly neighbor to support her meth addiction. The newspaper recounts the horrific details of the crime and paints the perpetrator with dark and demonic brush strokes, but just then—in the last few paragraphs of the article—you read a quote from Grandma, who just can't fathom how her grandbaby could do such a thing. "He never meant no harm." "She's still a good woman, ain't no one can take that from her."

What do we make of this? Is Grandma right? Can someone be both bad and good at the same time? Can a murderer still be a good person deep down, even though he strangled his own wife? Is it right to say that a child-beater is a good person? Doesn't it seem obvious that such folks are bad as bad can be? Well, that all depends on what kind of *good* we are talking about.

Philosophy is all about making distinctions. And this question about *the good person* is a philosophical question—it demands an important distinction about the good.

So let's make a distinction.

One type of good is *ontological* good. 'Ontological' goodness is just a fancy way of saying that goodness is rooted in the structure of reality, in the very nature of the thing itself. This is the type of good we hear about in the first creation story in the book of *Genesis*. Recall that at the end of each day God looks at what he has made and he calls it good. Everything God makes is good because God, who is all-good, made it to be good.

Since all of creation reflects God's goodness, the ocean, the sky, and the land are all ontologically good, even if the seas are rough, the sky is dark, and the land is dry—in and of themselves they remain good, because God made them. The same holds true for plants and animals. A poison ivy plant is good even if it gives me a rash, because it is part of God's creation. And even if my dog Fido makes a mess on my off-white sofa, and I say, "Bad dog! Bad dog!," philosophically and theologically speaking, Fido remains good, because God made him.

Like the rest of creation, human beings are also ontologically good. In fact, *Genesis* actually tells us that we humans are 'very good' since we are made in God's image and likeness. There is nothing we can do to take away this type of goodness. Human beings, by the fact that God made us, are good—*ontologically good*. According to this type of goodness, therefore, every person is a good person.

So what about the murderer and the child-beater? They may both be ontologically good by the very fact that God made them in His image and likeness, but surely there is something about them that is not good, isn't there?

We need to make another distinction.

There is another type of good—the *moral* good. Unlike other animals that act on instinct, we human beings (made in the image and likeness of God) are rational animals. We have an intellect and a will. Unlike every other animal, we can think—we can know that we know. We can also know the difference between good and bad, right and wrong, ugly and beautiful. Moreover, we have the ability to choose. We can choose God's will or our own. We can choose to act in love or in fear. We can choose to serve or to dominate. We can choose to forgive or to seek revenge. The kind of choices we make determine our moral goodness. In this sense, the woman who chooses to love and serve and forgive is 'a good person'—morally speaking. And the man who chooses against love, opting for a life of lust and revenge can rightfully be called 'a bad person'—morally speaking. *Moral good*, therefore, depends upon our ability to know what is good and to choose it.

So, is there such a thing as a bad person? Well, it all depends upon what you mean by *bad*. Ontologically bad? Impossible. Or morally bad? Possibly. The right answer all comes down to making the right distinction.

Chapter 11

Corpus Christi:
"Say 'Amen' to Who You Are!"

by Rev. Michael Woost

"Say 'Amen' to who you are!" The words of St. Augustine, the Bishop of Hippo, must have caused wonder and astonishment in his community. In the fourth century, as in the twenty-first century, Christians acknowledged the consecrated bread and wine as the Body and Blood of the Risen Lord with a resounding "Amen" as they received communion. Yet, in an Easter homily, Augustine asked the members of his community to recognize a further consequence of their "Amen." For Augustine, each Christian's "Amen" was more than just a public declaration of his or her personal belief in the Body and Blood of Christ. It was also the proclamation of their identity.

In the weeks following the Great Vigil of Easter, the neophytes—those who were newly initiated into the Church—engaged in a time of *mystagogia* (i.e., reflecting on the experience of sacramental-liturgical celebration). Augustine, like other pastoral leaders of Christian communities both past and present, called the neophytes to reflect upon "the mysteries," the liturgical rites, in which they had participated at the Easter Vigil. Having been immersed in the waters of baptism, sealed with oil in the act of chrismation, and invited to partake in the one bread and one cup, Augustine guided the neophytes as they unpacked their experience of the sacraments of Christian initiation. Sharing his homiletic reflections with them, Augustine no doubt drew upon insights from Scripture, the Church's tradition, and his own experience of initiation.

Augustine himself was a "catechumen" for almost thirty-three years prior to his baptism. Often marked by periods of religious inactivity and unfaithfulness, Augustine's early life was less than exemplary. However, once he made the decision to commit himself fully to Christ, a radical shift in his lifestyle occurred. Augustine understood this shift as coming from his own identification with Christ in love: "He loved us ungodly, to make us godly; loved us unrighteous, to make us righteous; loved us sick, to make us whole."[13] Incarnated in Jesus the Christ, revealed in the Scriptures, and embodied in the faith community, in Christians who became other Christs for him, the power of God's love effected a transformation in Augustine. When he was fully initiated into the Church by St. Ambrose at the Easter Vigil in 387, Augustine realized his new identity, joined to the life, death, and resurrection of Christ and incorporated into his Body, the Church. Augustine was one—one with the Father through Christ in the power of the Spirit and one with the Church community, forever covenanted in the bond of God's unfailing love.

---

[13] Augustine, "Homily IX on 1 John 4:17-21," trans. H. Browne, in *A Select Library of the Nicene and Post-Nicene Fathers of the Christian Church (First Series)*, ed. Philip Schaff, vol. 7 (Buffalo, NY: Christian Literature Co., 1888; reprint, Grand Rapids, MI: Wm. B. Eerdmans Publishing Co., 1986), 518.

It was this sense of identity, of oneness with Christ and his Church, that Augustine attempted to impress upon his own community at Hippo after he became its bishop in 395. It is not surprising then that his mystagogical reflections with the neophytes would turn to this theme. In one of his most often quoted homilies, Augustine tells the members of his community:

> These things ... are called sacraments for the reason that in them one thing is seen, but another is understood. That which is seen has physical appearances, that which is understood has spiritual fruit. If, then, you wish to understand the body of Christ, listen to the Apostle as he says to the faithful, "You are the body of Christ, and His members" (1 Cor. 12:27). If, therefore, you are the body of Christ and His members, your mystery has been placed on the Lord's table, you receive your mystery. You reply 'Amen' to that which you are, and by replying you consent. For you hear, "The Body of Christ," and you reply, "Amen." Be a member of the body of Christ so that your "Amen" may be true.[14]

The significance of these words is as frightening as it is astounding! Augustine is telling his community—and us: Not just bread and wine are placed upon the Lord's table. You are the sacrament laid on the altar of the Lord.

---

[14] Augustine, "Sermon 272" in *The Eucharist*, ed. Daniel J. Sheerin, Message of the Fathers of the Church, gen. ed. Thomas Halton, no. 7 (Wilmington, DE: Michael Glazier, Inc., 1986), 94-95.

It is here where our truest identity is revealed. You receive the sacrament of what you are. When you come to our Eucharist and are presented with the Body and Blood of the Lord, you are not just saying, "Amen, I believe this is the Body and Blood of Christ." You are saying, "Amen, *we* are the Body of Christ." You are saying, "Amen, in receiving the Body and Blood of the Lord, we are ever becoming His real presence in the world."

The consequences of our simple "Amen" are overwhelming. By his words, Augustine reminds us that, for Christians, Eucharist is not a noun, but a verb. Eucharist is not an object, but a way of life. In saying "Amen," we commit ourselves not just to receiving the Body of Christ, but also to living as the Body of Christ. Our sharing in Eucharistic communion commits us to living in communion with others—excluding no one because Christ's love knows no limits. At any Eucharistic liturgy, we pray, like Augustine's community, that our "Amen" may be authentic. May we live what we receive.

"Say 'Amen' to who you are!

Chapter 12

Tabernacles of Flesh and Blood

by Rev. Michael Woost

The celebration of Eucharist is more than consecrated bread and wine. I saw it enfleshed in the life of the Missionaries of Charity (MC) in India. Through the "Mother Teresa Project for Seminarians," three seminarians and I spent one month participating in the life of their community in Calcutta. Praying with the sisters and other volunteers from around the world, we experienced Eucharist in daily morning Mass and nightly Eucharistic Devotions.

With these liturgies framing their days, the Missionaries of Charity move from joyfully and reverently receiving Christ present in the Eucharistic species to joyfully and reverently touching the broken Body of Christ in the orphaned, the developmentally disabled, the leprous, the sick, and the dying – all "Christ in distressing disguise," as Mother Teresa said.

After two weeks of witnessing unimaginable poverty, of ministering at Mother Teresa's Home of the Dying Destitutes, and of praying each night after Benediction that Christ would be "loved, honored, and adored in every Tabernacle throughout the world," I proposed in a homily one morning at Mass that while there are many tabernacles made of precious metal, there are many more that are made of flesh and blood. The very act of consuming the Eucharistic Christ, I told the sisters, reminds us of whose and who we are as his Body. And certainly, ministering with them reminded me of how the very act of celebrating Eucharist should lead us to love, honor, and adore Christ in those flesh-and-blood tabernacles who are our sisters and brothers.

In a subsequent conversation, one of the sisters told me,

> Father, your reflections reminded me of things that Mother would say to us. Every time we opened a new house anywhere in the world, Mother said: "We've opened a new Tabernacle." For years the sisters thought that she meant we had established a new house with a new chapel and tabernacle containing the Eucharist. Then, one day, someone said something about this to Mother and she said: "No, the community of sisters is the new Tabernacle because that is where Jesus will be found."

This is Eucharist celebrated, received, adored, enfleshed, touched, and lived in community, service, and love. In celebration and service, the life of a Missionary of Charity is thoroughly Eucharistic. Yet, this is not just the MC way of life. This is our way of life as the Eucharistic community Christ calls us to be.

The bishops of the United States reaffirmed this in a document entitled *The Real Presence of Jesus Christ in the Sacrament of the Eucharist: Basic Questions and Answers.*

In championing Christ's presence in the Eucharist, our bishops present the Eucharist as a liturgical action directed to nourishing our participation in the life of the Trinity. However, they assert that, ". . . the celebration of the Eucharist does not just unite us to God as individuals who are isolated from one another."[15] Rather, ". . . we are united to Christ, together with all the other members of the Mystical Body."[16] The Eucharist should "increase our love . . . and remind us of our responsibilities toward one another."[17] These include representing Christ to the world; sharing the Gospel through word and daily living; and working against all that opposes the Gospel, ". . . including all forms of injustice."[18] Finally, quoting from *The Catechism of the Catholic Church*, our bishops note that, ". . . the Eucharist commits us to the poor."[19] By its very nature, Eucharist is a stinging condemnation of the radical individualism and privatism that often marks our society and can even affect our participation in the Church's liturgy.

---

[15] United States Conference of Catholic Bishops, *The Real Presence of Jesus Christ in the Sacrament of the Eucharist: Basic Questions and Answers* (Washington, D.C.: USCCB Publishing, 2001), 18 (question 14).

[16] Ibid.

[17] Ibid.

[18] Ibid.

[19] *The Catechism of the Catholic Church* (Vatican: Libreria Editrice Vaticana, 1994), art. 1397; quoted in United States Conference of Catholic Bishops, *The Real Presence of Jesus Christ in the Sacrament of the Eucharist: Basic Questions and Answers* (Washington, D.C.: USCCB Publishing, 2001), 18 (question 14).

With our bishops, I hope their teachings will lead us all to a deeper appreciation of the Eucharistic Mystery. I hope it will spur renewed interest in the Second Vatican Council's *Constitution on the Sacred Liturgy*, which stressed the unique presence of Christ in the Eucharist and reminded us of His presence in every sacrament, in the Word proclaimed, in the liturgy's presider, and in God's people gathered. I hope too that their words on responsibility will help us to enflesh what the Church's ritual, *Holy Communion and Worship of the Eucharist Outside Mass*, has already declared – namely, that our Eucharistic Devotions should lead us to ". . . be concerned with good deeds" so as to ". . . imbue the world with the Christian spirit and be a witness of Christ in the midst of human society."[20]

With the wisdom of grace, Mother Teresa formed a Eucharistic community and taught them to recognize the real presence of Christ in sacramental and human form. With her, may our Eucharist lead us to acclaim: "Blessed be Jesus in the most Holy Sacrament of the Altar." May our lives proclaim, as do the Missionaries of Charity every night by proclaiming a line Mother Teresa inserted into the *Divine Praises*: "Blessed be Jesus in the poorest of the poor."

---

[20] National Conference of Catholic Bishops, *Holy Communion and Worship of the Eucharist Outside Mass* (New York: Catholic Book Publishing Co., 1976), 65 (art. 81).

The Summertime of the Soul

Chapter 13

Summertime Leisure

by Sr. Mary McCormick, OSU

June is the month when people begin to shift into a different mode: summertime. Whether or not the details of your life are bounded by school schedules, there is a different pace of life during summer, especially for those of us who endure long, cold, snowy northeast Ohio winters.

There are numerous ways to define leisure, but in all ways it is related to happiness. Leisure is unoccupied time in which one can indulge in rest, recreation, and the pursuit of activities that enhance life. Leisure time enables us to transcend the routine of life so we can reflect on the import of things and perform significant acts. Leisure carries us to periods of delight in the ordinary and innocent pleasures of body and soul and to expression of creative energies.

From the perspective of Christian life, leisure is understood in the broad context of sacred time. The very first story in Genesis reminds us that time itself is sacred to God and that rest is included in the regular pace of life. Moreover, several places in the scripture encourage us to rest and seek God's favor by asking to be restored. For example, Psalm 80 continually repeats: "O Lord of hosts, restore us; let your face shine on us that we may be saved." Psalm 127 reminds us that in vain we "put off our rest." Jesus himself tells us: "Come to me, all you who labor and are burdened, and I will give you rest" (Mt:11:28).

In other words, the purpose of leisure activities is to promote the fullest self-realization of the individual. One of the documents of Vatican II, *Gaudium et Spes*, encourages this understanding of leisure: "May this leisure time be properly employed to refresh the spirit and strengthen the health of mind and body" (GS 61).

There is a connection between leisure and spirituality I think. When I talk about spirituality, I am informed by the thinking of Ronald Rolheiser in his book, *The Holy Longing*. Rolheiser believes that every person must have a spirituality, whether it be life-giving or destructive. He describes spirituality as what we do with the fire in our lives or with our deepest desires.

Leisure is connected to spirituality because in leisure time we have the opportunity to be attentive to what constitutes true human happiness. Because leisure is connected to spirituality, it is also connected to liturgy, i.e., it takes place in the rhythm of time. Keeping a rhythm of time is one way we humans respond to the repetition of every-day-ness. Leisure occurs when we interrupt the every-day-ness. In leisure we enter into life more fully. It provides us with the time to rest, be renewed and rekindle the relationships that give meaning to our lives.

The first thing we need to do is slow down. It is no novel insight to say that contemporary life is out of control with busy-ness.

When we take the time to slow down, to interrupt the hectic pace in which we usually live, we have the opportunity to develop a contemplative stance toward life. Renowned religious educator   Maria Harris describes contemplation as an uncluttered appreciation of existence, a state of mind or a condition of the soul that is simultaneously   wide-awake   and   free   from   all preoccupation, preconception, and interpretation.   That means, we take the time to look closely at the world around us and ponder the wonder of creation and the various creatures in the universe.

The philosopher Josef Pieper describes leisure as a condition of the soul. He suggests two ways for us to consider this. First, leisure is a "form of stillness that is the necessary preparation for accepting reality; . . . [it is] the recognition of the mysterious character of the world." Second, leisure is "the condition of considering things in a celebrating spirit."[21]

Let me suggest some ways this might be accomplished:

- Sit on the porch or in the backyard and visit with friends and family
- Go to your favorite beach, lake or riverside
- Watch the flames of a fire
- Look at the stars on a clear, dark night

---

[21] Josef Pieper, *Leisure, The Basis of Culture*, trans. G. Malsbary (South Bend, IN: St. Augustine's Press, 1998), 31, 50.

- Read a good book
- Plant and tend a garden
- Play with your children, your grandchildren, your nieces and nephews

The poet Gerard Manley Hopkins expresses it this way: ". . . for Christ plays in ten thousand places,/ Lovely in limbs and lovely in eyes not his."[22]

---

[22] See Gerard Manley Hopkins, "As Kingfishers Catch Fire," lines 12-13.

Chapter 14

Sabbath Rest

by Rev. Mark Latcovich

"There's not enough time in the day !" How often have we said this or heard others express this sentiment. Time "for just staying put" seems to be more of a sought-after luxury that is increasingly becoming absorbed by work, family commitments, meetings, appointments, personal errands and social engagements. And in the end, this is costing us—big time. I am not just talking about the rising cost of fuel, but in a more dramatic way, the cost of not taking the time necessary to cultivate our familial, cultural, social and religious lives (*CCC* #2184).

Maybe it's time to reclaim the Sabbath.

The Scriptures tell us, "And on the seventh day God finished the work he had done." When "[T]he heavens and earth were finished," God rested on this day and sanctified it and blest it," (Gen 2:1-3). Creation was fashioned with a Sabbath built into our weekly schedules. God gives us a period of time each week to receive the blessings of creation and redemption. One theologian notes that the weekly Sabbath is given to everyone as a free gift of equality that transcends social class and economic status. It is a day for worship. It is also a much needed day away from work

The *Catechism of the Catholic Church* notes that as Catholics we celebrate the Sabbath on Sunday, as a celebration of the resurrection of Christ. On Sunday, we rest from our weekly work and focus on our true "work"— the solemn worship of God (*CCC* #347).

Statistics tell us that regular church attendance is something that only about 20% of Americans do on a weekly basis. Recent studies tell us that about 23% of Catholics attend Mass each Sunday. Sadly, most people seem to substitute other weekly activities or use Sunday as "catch-up day" for work not finished during the week. As a result, they miss the richness and blessings that come from Sabbath rest! Let me explain what I mean. We sanctify the Sabbath when we consciously offer thanks to God and join him in his Sabbath rest. This rest is not seen in a literal way as extra time to catch up on sleep. Rather, it is weekly time afforded us to focus on a much bigger picture.

Each Sabbath invites us to rest as God rested from his work. In this rest, God reflects on the goodness of creation and fills it with his presence. We reflect on how God's presence fills our work and life, and we celebrate the blessings we have received as we delight in God's marvelous goodness to us. Christ rose on Sunday and offered us the mystery of redemption. Our celebration of the Sunday Eucharist allows us to participate in Christ's dying and rising, and it shapes our lives according to that mystery. We gather as a community to receive God's gifts of holiness and life bestowed on us through Christ's death and resurrection. Our Eucharistic worship is our testimony of belonging to, and being faithful to Christ and his Church as we strengthen one another under the guidance of the Spirit (*CCC* #2182).

Weekly church attendance is perhaps the best way to give a portion of our spirit and blessing to each other and the world as we celebrate our rising with Christ! This encourages us to let go of our personal concerns and worries, and withdraw from the cares which will not withdraw from us, so we can focus on others who may need our presence and prayers. We might hold in our hearts a line we heard from the gospel, think about the lesson learned from the homily, or keep humming that melody line from that hymn that seemed to calm our soul.

So what do we do after giving God the first few hours of our day? Maya Angelou suggests that a Sabbath rest gives us permission to retreat spiritually and seek refreshment for body, mind and spirit. She writes,

> Each of us needs hours of aimless wandering or spaces of time for sitting on a park bench, observing the mysterious world of ants and the canopy of treetops. Each deserves a day away in which no problems are confronted, no solutions searched for. If we step away for a time, we are not as many think and some will accuse, being irresponsible, but we are preparing ourselves to more ably perform our duties and discharge our obligations. A day away acts as a spring

tonic. It can dispel rancor, transform indecision and renew the spirit.[23]

Not bad advice for Catholics looking for a renewal of spirit each Sunday as we observe the Sabbath of the Lord.

---

[23] Maya Angelou, *Wouldn't Take Nothing for My Journey Now* (New York: Random House, 1993), 139.

Chapter 15

Aquinas and the Summertime Blues

by Rev. Damian Ference

It has been over fifty years since Eddie Cochran first proclaimed in his Top Ten hit that, "There ain't no cure for the summertime blues." But seven hundred years before Cochran, Saint Thomas Aquinas had come to a different conclusion. As a matter of fact, Thomas devotes an entire question of the *Summa Theologica* (I-II, 38, 1-5) to finding cures to the summertime blues - and to the Fall, Winter, and Springtime blues as well.

Thomas recognizes that part of our human condition is to experience sorrow and pain. In other words, no matter who we are, at some time in our life, we all get the blues. But what are we supposed to do when we are down? Is there a way out? Is there a remedy?

Thomas believes that there certainly is. Inspired by the works of Cicero, Aristotle, St. Ambrose, and St. Augustine, Thomas offers us five very practical cures for the summertime blues.

1. Pleasure: When we get down, Thomas suggests that one of the best things that we can do is partake in some activity that we enjoy. In other words, sitting around the house thinking about how depressed we are isn't much help. So, if you enjoy exercise, go out and take a run, or call a friend to play tennis or golf. If you like movies, watch a good movie, or if books are your thing, read a good book. The point is that it's important to get up and move – do something you enjoy. Of course, Thomas does not condone sinful activity, as that would only make matters worse. However, getting up and out and taking part in an activity that brings you pleasure and takes your mind off yourself for a while will help.

2. Tears: Thomas explains that crying is a remedy for the blues, and not just crying, but weeping and groaning as well. Often times we are embarrassed by our tears, and we can tend to think that crying is a sign of weakness. But Thomas argues that it is healthy to cry, weep, and groan, and that such acts actually lessen the burden of sorrow, since sorrow leaves our body through our tears. Thomas goes on to say that we human beings enjoy whatever comes naturally to us, and since it is natural for someone who is sad to cry, crying is a natural remedy to sorrow and pain. Anyone who has had a good cry recently can tell you how right Thomas is. Tears are cleansing, and crying just feels good. And of course, even Jesus wept, so that should tell us something.

3. Friends: If crying is good, then the only thing that makes it better is to have a good friend with you, rubbing your back and handing you tissues as you shed your tears. Since sorrow is like a weight that pushes us down, Thomas explains that good friends are able to help take some of that weight off our shoulders and lift us up. Moreover, Thomas observes that when our friends console us, we realize that we are loved by them, and this realization can help bring us out of our sorrow and pain, because we all need to be reminded that we are loved, especially when we're down.

4.   *Contemplation of Truth*: Often times we experience pain and sorrow because we have been duped. The world tells us that there is no truth, and we are constantly being bombarded with lies about who God is (or is not) and who we are. But God has placed a deep desire in every human heart to know the truth. Thomas tells us that we come to know the truth by way of faith and reason, and that contemplating truth is the greatest of all pleasures. Of course, Jesus is the Way, and the *Truth*, and the Life, and it is only Jesus that can ever truly satisfy our hungry hearts.

5. *Sleep & Baths*:   Of all the remedies Thomas offers, this final remedy is the most practical, and is also my personal favorite. Since sleep and baths help heal the body, Thomas wisely adds them to his list. He explains that whatever restores the body to its normal state will naturally drive away sorrow and pain. We all know how refreshing a good night's sleep can be, and who doesn't enjoy the relaxation offered by a warm bath or hot tub?

Thomas Aquinas is arguably the most prominent theologian and philosopher of our Catholic intellectual tradition, yet for this very reason, many everyday Catholics fear that his writings might be over their heads. But we shouldn't fear Thomas; he is our friend. He is a saint who speaks to all people on all sorts of topics - even on finding cures for the summertime blues.

Chapter 16

Handing on the Faith

By Sr. Mary McCormick, OSU

W hen summer is over, and people start thinking about returning "back to school," a different pace comes as people return to a more "usual" schedule. Yes, it affects schools, but it also affects the pace of parish life.

It provides a good opportunity to reflect on handing on faith. Church documents remind us that parents are the first and primary teachers of faith.[24] But all of the baptized have a shared responsibility in handing on faith to those in our faith community, with the parish as the particular locus for that activity.[25]

Let me explain what I mean. In part, I am referring to the formal aspect of handing on faith. Earlier centuries referred to this as the *fides quae*, i.e., the objective content of faith or what the church believes. Certain people within each parish have a specific responsibility for this among whom are the pastor, the

---

[24] See Vatican II's *Declaration on Christian Education*, #3 and the *General Directory for Catechesis*, #226-227.
[25] See *General Directory for Catechesis*, #253-264

director of faith formation, the Catholic school principal and teachers, parish catechists, members of the youth ministry team and RCIA team.

The Catholic Church has a broad, rich heritage of faith developed over centuries. The Church has both the catechetical vision and elements of the curriculum that guide diocesan and parish leaders in a sequence for nurturing the young people in the content of the faith. We rightly take pride in helping others within our community to learn more about this tradition of faith.

But there is another element of the life of faith that is also important. It is the response one makes to the mystery of life and the awareness that God is present to us in our lives. Earlier centuries referred to this as the *fides qua*, i.e., the response in faith by which one turns to God in Christ and the Spirit through one's acceptance of what the Church believes.

These two elements of the life of faith are complementary to one another. For example, when a young person recognizes strong faith in another because she perceives a deep sense of respect for human life, or a commitment to charity and justice, or strength of character (*fides qua*), it may inspire her to inquire more about that faith (*fides quae*).

It is in the *fides qua* where the whole Christian community has a special responsibility. In every aspect of our lives, we have the opportunity and potential to give personal witness to our response to God's presence at work within us. This can happen both in the parish and in the larger world and can take many forms. Within the parish one can fully, actively, and consciously participate in liturgy, get involved in charitable activities like feeding the hungry or visiting the sick, and engage in works of justice which aim to get at the causes of social problems. Outside the parish one can demonstrate one's respect for and the dignity of each human person in conversation and behavior, one can make decisions that reflect Christian moral principles, and avoid the temptation to cut corners in the quality of work. When we live our lives in a conscious response to God's presence in our midst, it might inspire others to learn more about the faith that motivates our lives.

No matter what our age, each of us can take advantage of learning more about our shared faith. At both the parish and the diocesan level, there are numerous opportunities to be life-long learners in various aspects of our Catholic heritage. Moreover, Catholic books, periodicals, audio tapes, DVDs, and websites expand our exposure to faith formation.

In 2012, all of us were invited to engage both of these aspects of faith, the *fides quae* and the *fides qua*, as we prepared for and began using, the new Roman Missal. It was an opportunity for all of us to learn more about the elements of the Mass, the historical context in which this change occurred and the theological notions expressed in the new words for our prayer. All of this was part of our developing *fides quae*.

At the same time, it was an opportunity for us to witness to one another how change is received among Catholics. At first the language seemed odd. No doubt there were moments of awkwardness and mistakes. But an attitude of openness to God's presence in these words at this time in our history could provide the moral support we need to move gracefully into this new era of our heritage. This is an example of *fides qua*, making a response of faith in light of the content of faith.

Even though many at Mass may not have noticed it, both aspects of faith, the *fides quae* and the *fides qua*, were quietly at work, deepening their spiritual lives as they prayed.

Section IV

Spirituality

Chapter 17

Coincidence?

by Dr. Edward Kaczuk

"For the Christian, there are no coincidences," states a colleague of mine occasionally in his homilies. The thought can seem so theoretical—until it becomes a startling reality in life.

In the last month or so of the 2003-2004 school year, I began to hear a voice telling me to affirm a particular student. The voice was persistent, but I was not. Before I knew it, the school year was over and I had not accomplished my task. As I left the reception following Commencement Exercises on the last day of school in May, there was the student, standing alone by the doorway. This time I didn't miss the perfect opportunity and told him what was on my mind. It was clear to me that this encounter was not happenstance.

Another 'coincidence' occurred in the process of the sale of my mom's house, when the closing date was set for the second anniversary of my dad's death in February. As we visited our home for the last time a few days before the closing, I reflected on the love of God that had enveloped us since my dad's death. No fluke here in the timing of the sale.

Then I read the *Newsweek* issue commemorating Pope John Paul II. It quoted John Paul in a highlighted box, "In the designs of Providence, there are no mere coincidences." Was this just coincidence?

This is another way of stating the sacramental principle: everything potentially mediates grace. "Grace super-abounds," stated St. Paul (Rom. 5:15). St. Thomas Aquinas said that one cannot distinguish the causes of an event by ascertaining our action as opposed to natural causes and God's action. God is the source of all natural causes because God loves all of creation completely, absolutely and perfectly at every moment and holds it in being. St. Thérèse of Lisieux was last able to receive communion about six weeks prior to her death. This did not sadden her. She said, "No doubt it is a great grace to receive the sacraments. When God does not permit it, it is good too! Everything is a grace."

The attempt on Pope John Paul's life turned into a profound moment of grace as John Paul forgave his would-be assassin, Mehmet Ali Agca, in a prison cell. The debilitating effects of Parkinson's disease on the once athletic body of John Paul could certainly be viewed as a tragedy. It enabled him, however, to give powerful witness to the value of each human life and the value of connecting one's sufferings to the mystery of the cross in the final days, weeks and months of his papacy.

Theologian Michael Himes, of Boston College, defines the sacramental principle in this way, "That which is always and everywhere the case goes unnoticed unless it is expressed and celebrated somewhere and sometime." In his poem "Hurrahing in Harvest," the 19th century Jesuit poet Gerard Manley Hopkins said "These things, these things were here and but the beholder wanting." The moments that we become beholders, the occasions that lead us to notice the presence of the love of God are sacraments. Sacraments are occasions, persons, places, things and events that lead us to notice the presence of the perfect love of God for us. Certainly they include "the seven great Sacraments," and also countless personal sacraments, such as your spouse, your children, and your parents. Even sin may lead to grace, as we pray in the Easter *Exsultet*, "O truly necessary sin of Adam . . . O happy fault that earned so great, so glorious a Redeemer!"

One of the gifts that the ordained minister as homilist gives is to point out moments of grace in the life of the community. It is a gift that of all of us are capable of giving. Seek to behold the moments of grace in your own life, look for them and point them out in the lives of those around you. You'll discover the most amazing things.

Coincidence? I think not.

Chapter 18

Speaking Prophetically

by Rev. John Loya

When we were baptized, we were anointed a priestly people, a prophetic people and a royal people. As a priestly people we are to have a sacrificial love for others in memory of Christ's sacrificial love for us in the Eucharist. As a royal people we lay down our lives serving one another in memory of Christ the King who washed his disciples' feet at the Last Supper. As a prophetic people Christ has given us the mission to proclaim the Gospel to all nations.

According to the Scripture scholar Walter Brueggemann, "The task of prophetic ministry is to nurture, nourish, and evoke a consciousness and perception alternative to the consciousness and perception of the dominant culture around us," (*The Prophetic Imagination*). In other words, when "everybody" is saying one thing, the prophet proclaims something different. Many times this prophetic alternative is just the opposite of what the dominant culture says is true. To help us discern a cultural perspective from a prophetic one, we can use an ancient wisdom story as a discernment tool:

> The disciple couldn't wait to tell the Master the rumor he had heard in the marketplace.

"Wait a minute," said the Master. "What you plan to tell us, is it true?"

"I don't think it is," replied the disciple.

"Is it useful?" asked the Master.

"No, it isn't" said the disciple.

"Is it funny?" inquired the Master.

"No" said the disciple.

"Then why should we be hearing it?" said the Master.[26]

Applying the three questions: "Is it true?" "Is it useful?" and "Is it funny?" to a statement, and answering any of the three questions in the affirmative will indicate whether or not the statement is a prophetic alternative. For example: "Time heals all wounds." Is it true? According to the Gospel, the answer is "no." Did time or Jesus heal the woman who suffered from a hemorrhage for twelve years? Did time or Jesus heal the man who had been at the Pool of Bethesda for thirty-eight years? Did time or Jesus heal the man born blind? Is the saying "Time heals all wounds" useful? The answer is also "no." Following this advice a wounded individual could bleed to death without medical care before time had time to heal the wound. Lastly, this saying is certainly not funny. A prophetic alternative might be: "Time heals nothing. Time ages and, thus, turns new wounds into old wounds. Jesus Christ heals--naturally, sacramentally, miraculously or through the gift of medicine."

St. Paul advises us prophets to "test everything; retain what is good." (I Thes. 5:21). Let us not be afraid to

[26] Anthony de Mello, SJ, *One Minute Wisdom* (New York: Doubleday, 1985), 28.

question perspectives we have always thought to be true because "everybody" says so. Below are just a few of the thousands of things "everybody" in the dominant culture is saying as well as some possible prophetic alternatives. With prophetic courage examine each of them and discover which are true, which are useful, and which are funny.

Cultural Voice: "Variety is the spice of life."

Prophetic Voice: Variety is a sign of wealth. Gratitude is the spice of life.

Cultural Voice: "There are good days and bad days."

Prophetic Voice: There are good days and hard days. God doesn't create any bad days.

Cultural Voice: "Love is a feeling."

Prophetic Voice: Love is not a feeling. Love is patient. Love is kind.

Cultural Voice: Seek loving relationships.

Prophetic Voice: If you love those who love you, what merit is there in that? Seek first the Kingdom of God.

Cultural Voice: "Words have power."

Prophetic Voice: Words have meaning. The Word of God has the Power.

Cultural Voice: "The Bill of Rights gives us the right to abortion."

Prophetic Voice: God gives everyone, born and unborn, the right to life.

Let your faith assist you in distinguishing the true, the useful and the funny from the false, the useless and the tragic.

Chapter 19

Physical or Spiritual Hunger?

by Rev. John Loya

T wo women who were life-long friends decided to go on a diet in order to lose a few pounds. By supporting each other in sticking to a diet program both reached their goal weight in no time. After several months, however, the first woman began to put unwanted pounds back on while the second managed to maintain her desired weight. Frustrated, the first woman went to her friend and said, "What is your secret? How do you keep yourself from gaining weight? I find myself eating when I am not even hungry."

Her friend replied, "I have learned that we do not only have bodies that get hungry but we also have souls that get hungry too. When I feel hungry and my body has had its allotted amount of food, I know that it is not my body that is hungry. It is my soul. I give my soul the nourishment it needs by taking a walk, meditating or reading a good book."

One of the reasons why most diets do not work is that they fail to address our spiritual hunger. If we are unaware that our souls can get just as hungry as our bodies, we frequently mistake one hunger for another.

Thinking that we are physically hungry when we are really spiritually hungry, we can end up stuffing our bodies with food it does not need while starving our souls of food it cannot live without. When we treat our spiritual hunger as if it is a physical hunger, we neglect our deeper hungers that manifest themselves in such ways as disappointment, discouragement, fear and loneliness. We will never satisfy the soul's spiritual hunger and thirst by consuming physical food and drink. Since our spiritual hunger is a real hunger, we need real food for our souls. Fortunately for us, God supplies us with all the spiritual food we need. The Living Father has sent the Son to feed us. The soul-food Christ gives us is the Bread of Life which has come down from heaven. The Body of Christ is real food and the Blood of Christ is real drink. Our spiritual hunger for eternal life is satisfied in eating this true food and true drink (John 6).

The saying, "We are what we eat" is true not only for physical food, but also for spiritual food. The reason the Son of God became human was that we might become divine as Christ is (St. Athanasius, *De Incarnatione*). Consuming the Bread of Life, Christ's life becomes our life. Symbolized in washing his disciples' feet, Christ's life is a life of service to us. (John 13) In eating the Bread of Life, we become bread for each other through lives of service. Our spiritual hunger for love is satisfied through the laying down of our lives in love of others. Our spiritual hunger for peace and loving union is satisfied by believing in Jesus Christ.

By believing in the Bread of Life, by believing in the Christ who is Risen from the dead and who is with us always, we have eternal life (John 20). Believing in Christ means we never eat a meal alone for Christ is with us. We can never go for a solitary walk without Christ being at our side. We can never be all alone in a room anymore because Christ is right there with us.

Unless we eat the Bread of Life, we will not have eternal life in us but we will have eternal hunger. Taking in the Bread of Life, we take in the Christ who lives within us and satisfies the deepest hungers and longings of our minds, hearts and souls. Believing that the Risen Christ is with us always, we feed our souls with the real food and real drink, the Bread of Life, and become lives given in loving service of our neighbors.

Chapter 20

How To Change One's Feelings

By Rev. John Loya

How are you feeling? According to the News media Monday, January 6, 2014 is the most depressing day of that year, the bluest of Blue Mondays of the new year. Why? The Christmas holidays are over. New Year's resolutions are broken. Bills are arriving and the weather is unrelentingly cold. Is there any way of improving our emotional life at this or any other time of the year?

Yes, there is.

Our minds are like gardens. They can contain a wide variety of "plants," that is, beliefs, thoughts, interpretations or self-talk. Normally these "plants" are the cause of our emotions.[27] True beliefs and rational thoughts, "wheat," cause us to have positive emotions, that is, feelings we like. False beliefs and irrational thoughts,

_____

[27] These reflections exclude unusual situations where one's feelings may result from physical difficulties, the use of drugs, and the like.

"weeds," cause us to have negative emotions, that is, feelings we do not like. We can distinguish beliefs that are "wheat" from those that are "weeds" by employing the gifts of faith and reason, and by applying:

The Five Criteria of Rationality

1. Is this belief (or interpretation) objectively true?

2. Is this belief life preserving?

3. Will this belief help me to reach my goal as quickly and as easily as possible?

4. Will this belief help me to avoid significant internal conflict?

5. Will this belief help me to avoid significant external conflict?[28]

When we are experiencing feelings we do not like, as does Joey in the following story, we can change our feelings by using the gifts of faith and reason.

Seven-year-old Joey was in the kitchen as his mother made supper. She asked him to go into the pantry and get her a can of tomato soup. Joey did not want to go in alone. He said, "It is dark in there and I am scared. " She asked again and he refused again. Finally she said, "It is O.K. Jesus will be in there with you." Joey walked hesitantly to the door and slowly opened it. He peeked inside and saw it was dark. Joey started to leave when all

---

[28] Denis Dougherty, "Pastoral Counseling: A Christian Application of Rational Emotive Therapy," Cassette Tapes, visual aid (Kansas City: National Catholic Reporter Publishing Company), 3.

at once an idea came, and he said, "Jesus, if you are in there, would you hand me that can of tomato soup?"

Joey's feeling of fear is caused by his belief that something intent on harming him, such as a monster or a zombie, is lurking in the dark pantry. If we apply the Five Criteria of Rationality to Joey's belief we make a remarkable and valuable discovery.

Is Joey's belief objectively true? No. Is his belief life preserving? No. Does his belief help him to reach his goal of a can of tomato soup? No. Does his belief enable him to avoid internal conflict with fear? No. Does his belief help him to avoid external conflict with his mother? No. All these negative answers indicate that Joey's belief is irrational and it will do him no earthly or heavenly good to continue believing it.

Because Joey is the one who controls his thoughts, he has a choice. He can foolishly cling to his irrational and false belief and continue to experience negative feelings. Or he can choose to believe that Jesus is with him, as his mother instructed him, and use reason to see that there is nothing in the pantry to be afraid of. By ridding his mind of a "weed," a false and irrational belief, and replacing it with "wheat," a true and rational belief, Joey effectively exchanges a negative feeling (fearful) for a positive one (confident) and is blessed with a more purposeful and fulfilling life.

The garden of our minds needs to be weeded of its false beliefs and irrational thinking. This is a task that must be done daily. We all know what happens to a garden that is left untended. The weeds eventually take over, and the garden is lost. To prevent this from happening to you, be patient and persistent in pulling out the weeds one at a time and replacing them with true beliefs and rational thoughts. You will not regret the time and effort you put into this liberating work.

Every year can be a Happy New Year filled with the Peace of Christ that comes from faith in Him and from the positive feelings that are caused by true beliefs and rational thinking.

Chapter 21

Catching a Glimpse of God's Love

By Rev. Mark Latcovich

T he 15th Century Russian Icon, painted by Andrei Rublev, depicts three angels seated around a table on which there is a Eucharistic cup. In the background, there is a house and a tree. This icon is inspired from the Scripture of Genesis 18, the visit of the three strangers to Abraham and Sarah. Abraham met the strangers outside, and despite not knowing their identity he called upon Sarah, who showed them extraordinary hospitality. While the visitors reclined under the oaks of Mamre, Sarah baked bread and Abraham prepared the meal. In the process of sharing the resources of the household, the identity of the visitors was revealed to be the Lord and two angels. The Lord then promised that the elderly Sarah and Abraham would have a child, Isaac.

The gesture of hospitality and one's own household and table become the setting in which Rublev crafts his artistic presentation of the Trinity. His artistic theology symbolizes some rather unique glimpses into the mystery of God. First, the oak tree stands for the tree of life. Second, the figures are arranged in a circle that is not closed. The seated figures invite the stranger to sit with them and be a part of their communion. This is an icon of hospitality, representing a God who is for us, a God not self-contained, but always inviting. This is not an image of closed society, but one that is inviting all to join and be a part of the table and share in the cup that is central to the image.

This icon expresses the fundamental insight of the Doctrine of the Trinity, namely that God is not far from us but lives among us in the communion of persons. Yet, this divine community formed by their relations to one another and to us, is often lost in our spiritual life and in our personal relationship with God. Catholics, like other Christians, do not always imagine God in a Trinitarian way. Karl Rahner, in his book on the Trinity, asserts that most Christians are monotheists, that is to say, Christians think of God as a single benevolent entity acting in the affairs of the world. This image of God forfeits the Christian's reflection of the true relational communion within God's self.

Popular piety sometimes describes God as a static entity acting as some spiritual energy or higher power in the universe. God is depicted as one force in the world. Yet this is not really the Christian doctrine of God. The revealed truth is that God is a Trinity! This truth is continuously reflected in the liturgy and prayers of the Church. For example, we imagine the Father's role in salvation history as the act of creation. God is also present in the continued activity of Jesus, as the new Adam of the new creation. In the Nicene Creed, we profess God the Spirit to be the Lord and Giver of life, sent to us by the Father and the Son. We remember Jesus' salvific action on the cross in our Eucharistic prayers, while celebrating the role of the Father and the Spirit in this act of redemption.

The *Catechism of the Catholic Church* states that, "The Mystery of the Trinity is the central mystery of the Christian faith and life. It is the mystery of God in God's own self. It is therefore the source of all other mysteries of faith and the light that enlightens them" (*CCC* #234). How can the doctrine of the Trinity illuminate our everyday lives? We are called to live a Trinitarian faith in the Church's prayer and in our everyday lives.

The late Trinitarian scholar Catherine Mowry LaCugna describes what it means to live Trinitarian faith in her book *God for Us*. Her ideas offer a summary of what it means to be baptized into the very life of God.

> Led by the Spirit more deeply into the life of Christ, we see the unveiled face of the living God. God's glory is beheld in Jesus Christ who is the instrument of our election, our adoption as daughters and sons of God, our redemption through his blood, the forgiveness of our sins, and the cause of our everlasting inheritance of glory ... [29]

When we try to live our lives around the mystery of the Trinity, we imagine the Father as the origin of love that reaches outward as a caring God, who, like a mother, never abandons her children and does everything, including sacrificing her life for the sake of the children.

---

[29] Lacugna, Catherine Mowry, *God For Us: The Trinity and the Christian Life* (New York: Harper Collins Publishers, 1991), 378.

God is the Father of us all, who is the essence of a caring, merciful Father, embracing the prodigal son, and the poor and marginalized as well.

Living Trinitarian faith means living as Jesus lived; preaching the Gospel, relying only on God, offering healing and reconciliation, rejecting laws that bind and impair, resisting temptations, embracing the enemy and the sinner, and surrendering oneself for the sake of the gospel on various levels of our lives.

Living Trinitarian faith means living in the power and presence of the Holy Spirit, training the eyes of the heart on God's face and name proclaimed before us in history; sharing in the creative life of God that raises Jesus from the dead, and inaugurates a sacramental life for the church. Living in the Spirit allows us be continuously created by the fire of divine love. These tongues of flame continue to fall on all of us as the fire of prophecy that inspires, refreshes and empowers human hearts to imitate God's passion.

The fiery tongues of Pentecost continue in the Church to send disciples on mission, and to stir up individuals and communities to become more God-like, God-filled and live as God's households. Trinitarian faith allows the spirit to dissolve boundaries, forgive sins, instill charisms and re-created that which is old, tired, dried or buried. Living as daughters and sons of the Trinity allows us to embracing true worship and become people of thanksgiving.

Chapter 22

Sing with All the Saints in Glory

By Rev. Mark Hollis

A s a priest, I can honestly say there was quite a bit of excitement on the day copies of the new third edition of the Roman Missal arrived. One element of the Roman Missal raised a great deal of interest in me. As I paged through the liturgical texts of some of the saints presented in the new Missal, I recognized names of those who have been canonized since the last edition of the Roman Missal which was issued in 1969. These words from the book of Book of Revelation came to me immediately:

> After this I saw before me a huge crowd which no one could count from every nation, people and tongue. They stood before the throne and the Lamb, dressed in long white robes and holding palm branches in their hands. They cried out in a loud voice, "Salvation is from our God, who is seated on the throne and from the Lamb. (Rev. 7:9-10)

In the third edition of the Roman Missal, for the first time, several celebrations of saints and other feasts are now included. The names of these holy men and women are indeed representative of "every nation, people and tongue." Here are just a few of the saints whose feast days are included.

St. *Josephine Bakhita, Virgin* (1869-1947) celebrated on February 8th. This holy woman was born in the Darfur region of Sudan in 1869. Sold into slavery as a young girl, Josephine eventually came to live in Venice, Italy where she gained her freedom and was introduced to the Catholic faith. Bakhita ("Fortunate" in Arabic) entered the catechumenate and subsequently received the sacraments of initiation in January, 1890. Three years later she entered the novitiate of the Conossian Sisters. She spent the rest of her life in Italy, other than three years in which she trained young women religious for work in Africa. As she grew older Mother Josephine suffered many illnesses. She died on February 8, 1947 and was canonized October 1, 2000.

St. *Pio of Pietrelcina, Priest* (1887-1968) celebrated on September 23rd. Padre Pio was born Francesco Forgione on May 25, 1887. This well-known Italian Capuchin focused his entire priestly ministry on the Sacrament of Reconciliation and the celebration of the Eucharist. Among the many people who visited with the saintly Capuchin was a young Polish priest, Fr. Karol Wojytla, who later became Pope John Paul II. St. Pio committed himself to relieving the pain and suffering of many families, chiefly through the foundation of the Casa Sollievo della Sofferenza (House for the Relief of Suffering), opened on 5 May 1956.

From his youth, his health was not very robust, and especially in the last years of his life it declined rapidly. On the day after the fiftieth anniversary of his receiving the stigmata (i.e., the wounds of Christ), he was extremely tired. Having renewed his Franciscan vows and made his final confession, Padre Pio died on 23 September 1968 at the age of eighty-one. He was beatified in 1999 and canonized by Pope John Paul II in 2002.

These two saints come from different continents and different backgrounds. Yet they remind us of the constellation of holy men and women of every time and place who have heard the call of the Lord and followed Him.

Continuing our "walk" through the Roman Missal we encounter men and women who had a love for the poor, simplicity of life, great devotion to the saints, as well as purity of life and love for Christ and the Church. Here are more of these newly added saints.

St. Andre Bessette, Religious (1845-1937) celebrated on January 6th. This Holy Cross Brother humbly cared for the poor in Montreal. The Oratory that he built in honor of St. Joseph was solemnly dedicated in 1955, and raised to the rank of a minor basilica. St. Andre was canonized on October 17, 2010

St. Katherine Drexel, Virgin (1858-1955) celebrated on March 3rd. Katharine Mary Drexel was born in Philadelphia, Pennsylvania where her family held a considerable fortune from banking. Her decision to become a Sister of Mercy shocked the social circles of Philadelphia. In addition to the vows of poverty, chastity and obedience, she added a fourth: "To be the mother and servant of the Indian and Negro races." She founded the Sisters of the Blessed Sacrament. St. Katharine Drexel was canonized October 1, 2000.

Saint Kateri Tekakwitha, Virgin (1656-1680) July 14th. Born in what is now the State of New York, this Native American persevered in her desire to become a Christian. She was baptized by Jesuit missionaries at the age of 20, living a virtuous life until her death from tuberculosis in 1680.

These are just a few of the saints whose feasts are now included in the Roman Missal. May our voices be joined to all the saints in heaven in a hymn of praise: "Holy, Holy, Holy Lord, God of hosts. Heaven and earth are full of your glory!"

Liturgical Life

Chapter 23

Glorifying the Lord by Your Life

by Damian J. Ference

The new translation of the Roman Missal, introduced during Advent of 2011, offers four options for the final dismissal at Mass. I want to take a good look at the third option, because it reminds us just what Mass and life is all about—"Go in peace, glorifying the Lord by your life."

Each and every time we celebrate the Eucharist, we accept God's invitation to save us, to change us, and to make us more like him. In the Penitential Rite, we recognize that we are sinners in order to prepare ourselves to listen to God speak to us in the Liturgy of the Word. Then we move to the altar, where bread and wine are changed into the body and blood of Jesus, which we are invited to eat and drink—not because we are worthy, but because God makes us worthy. And finally, we are sent: "Go in peace, glorifying the Lord by your life."

But here's the thing: we are not sent out to the world as the same people we were at the beginning of the Mass. The Mass should change us.

Acknowledging our sins should change us. Reminding ourselves that God is God, and that we are not, re-orders us. Recognizing the fact that Christianity is not a self-help religion, but calls us to realize our need for a

Savior should change us. Remembering that salvation comes from God and not from us should change us.

And what if God talked directly to us? What if we could hear his voice? In a real way, this is what happens at every Mass when we listen to the scriptures proclaimed— we hear the story of our salvation—we hear God tell us how much he loves us. And this should change us.

Then there is the most obvious change in the Eucharist. By his ordination, an unworthy servant stands in the place of Jesus Christ, the high priest, and calls down the Holy Spirit to change simple gifts of bread and wine into the body and blood of Jesus Christ. And this should change us.

God speaks to us in his Word so that we may be changed and become more like him. God gives us the gift of his Son in the Eucharist so that we might become like Jesus, or more boldly, that we might become him—*alter Christus*—another Christ. In other words, we are what we eat. If we eat unhealthy foods, we become unhealthy. If we eat healthy foods, we become healthy. If we eat the body and blood of Jesus Christ, we become Jesus.

This sort of thing sounds a bit heretical at first. How can we, a community of sinners, become *other Christs*? We can't do anything to make this happen – and this is the point: it isn't *what we do,* but *what God does* for us. As St. Anthanasius wrote, "God becomes man so that man can become God."[30] God saves us by changing us from

---

[30] Athanasius, *Treatise on the Incarnation of the Word*, trans. W. A. Jurgens (Collegeville: The Liturgical Press, 1970), 322.

sinners into saints. He gives us the body and blood of his Son to save us, to change us.

Now we can turn to the third option for the dismissal at the end of Mass, "Go in peace, glorifying the Lord by your life." Once we've been changed (by God) through our full, conscious, and active participation in the Mass, we are sent out into the world on mission. And our mission is to consecrate the world. By our baptismal priesthood, we are all sent out as other Christs to consecrate the little pockets of the world in which we dwell—our homes, schools, offices, factories, hospitals, parks, ball fields, construction sites, and every other place that we go. We are told to go in peace, a peace that only Christ can give—a peace that Christ gives us so that we can give his peace to others. We are told to glorify the Lord with our lives, which is so very beautiful, and so very Catholic, and so very Incarnational. In other words, the Church entrusts us with living our lives in such a way that our witness becomes an act of praise, a glorification of the Trinity.

When we glorify the Lord with our lives, we allow God to Incarnate himself in us—to manifest his presence in us. The saints all knew this—it is a big part of what makes them saints. Their witness brings God glory. They allow the Eucharist to change them so much that they become other Christs, and so change the world.

Of course, our baptism calls us to be saints too, and so does the Mass. The new translation, especially the third dismissal option, makes it clear that if the only thing that changes at Mass is the bread and wine, then something is terribly wrong.

Chapter 24

The Power of Symbol

By Dr. Edward Kaczuk

O n a Friday evening in July, en route to our favorite vacation spot on the Delaware shore, my family and I breezed through Washington, D.C. We found a parking spot on the Mall, near the Washington Monument, and walked off past a number of softball games to visit the Vietnam Veterans Memorial, "The Wall." Maya Ying Lin, then a young architecture student from Yale designed this monument, chosen from over 1,400 entrants in the public competition. Dedicated on Veterans Day in 1982, it was controversial because of its non-traditional appearance. Some veterans felt it did not convey the heroism, patriotism and honor inherent in most war memorials. This minimalist monument has proven to be powerfully evocative to the pilgrims who come daily.

On this particular day a group had just finished attending a ceremony, and was approaching the Wall. They had rubbings of names made, took pictures, gently touched the engraving of a name, left flowers, notes and pictures. I'd witnessed these scenes before at the Wall, but this time was different. Sons and daughters, nephews and nieces of those who had fallen were now 30-something-year-old men and women. Spouses and veterans were now in their fifties. As they related with the Wall and supported each other, I gained yet another perspective on this war. The polished black granite of the two 250-foot walls of the V-shaped memorial reflected back the images of all of us, telling us something about ourselves as well. As the design jury that chose Maya Ying Lin as the architect noted, the Vietnam Veterans Memorial was, and continues to be, ". . . a place of quiet reflection, and a tribute to those who served their nation in difficult times."[31] I left the monument, yet again changed by the encounter.

The next day at the ocean I would forget all about my day job, while jumping in waves that, frankly, at times were big enough to scare the bejeebers out of me. But, on this night at "The Wall," as we returned to our car, past the now ending softball games, I found myself drawing many comparisons between the power of this wall and the power of liturgical symbols.

Symbols convey a wealth of meaning. A symbol can speak to a wide variety of people in a wide variety of ways. Maya Ying Lin ". . . cut open the earth" to build the Wall as a symbol of death, ". . . a sharp pain that lessens with time, but can never quite heal over."[32] Others see the design as being a sheltered place set apart, or reflecting our country's gradual descent into the depths of the war. Liturgically, the waters of Baptism signify danger, destruction and death, leading to life, refreshment, healing and cleansing. These elements symbolize Baptism's range of theological meaning, burial with Christ so that we may

---

[31]http://www.everydaycitizen.com/2008/05/maya_lin
[32] Ibid.

rise with him, new life in Christ, healing and cleansing from sin.

This wealth of meaning makes rational explanations inadequate. Symbols convey meaning that is not accessible in any other way. You can't understand the power of The Wall until you have experienced it. The theology of Baptism may be explained to a catechumen, but the full meaning needs to be experienced by being plunged into water and being brought forth. This, I think, is why The Wall was initially controversial. One could not understand the power of this non-traditional monument by simply looking at the architect's sketch or reading about the design. One cannot understand the power of liturgical symbols without experiencing them over time. That is why a change in architecture for a worship space or ritual changes, such as those brought about by the new *Roman Missal,* while sometimes controversial, are eventually experienced as powerful.

A symbol makes present what it represents and leads us to a new reality. For many, as they encounter the Wall, the presence of the people whose names are on the wall is real. For me, the walk to the depth of the monument is a walk into that tortured time of our history. The encounter changes us, leads us to healing. Liturgically, Christ is present in the bread and wine when we celebrate Eucharist and that presence transforms us.

The catalyst for all these musings, the actions of veterans, widows, sons and daughters, as they related to this symbol, brought a different perspective and new meanings to me. Liturgically, people sharing in the Body and Blood of Christ, the young and the old kneeling to venerate the Cross on Good Friday, the face of the catechumen turned neophyte emerging from the water add to the power of these symbols.

As I body-surfed in the ocean water on the following day, bringing a hint of danger and yet refreshment to me, I really wasn't far from my day job after all.

Chapter 25

Why Is Mass So Boring?

by Rev. Gerald J. Bednar, Ph.D.

Sometimes people compare the Mass to what might be called "secular liturgies" like college football games. They each follow time-honored scripts, complete with detailed directions or "rubrics." On game day, students join together in their fight songs, perform quaint traditions, sing their Alma Mater, and chant various cheers in hopes of a victory. Win or lose, by the end of the day the student body has achieved a renewed sense of unity.

I would like to suggest that such comparisons to the Mass miss the mark. The college football game has much more in common with some pagan rituals than with Christian liturgies.

Take, for example, a "liturgy" reported by James Fenimore Cooper in his classic, *The Last of the Mohicans*. The Mohican Chief directs three warriors to strip the bark off of a small tree, to rip its branches off, and to color the tree red. This mutilated red-hued tree becomes an effigy of the enemy. A war song follows as the Indians join in a frenzied dance. Cooper writes, "It . . . awakened all the slumbering passions of a nation. A hundred youths, who had hitherto been restrained by the diffidence of their years, rushed in a frantic body on the . . . [effigy], and severed it asunder."[33]

Christian liturgies are not supposed to whip us up; they're supposed to calm us down.

Consider a passage from Isaiah that has traditionally been applied to Jesus: "He shall bring forth justice to the nations not crying out, not shouting, not making his voice heard in the street. A bruised reed he shall not break, and a smoldering wick he shall not quench, until he establishes justice on the earth" (Is. 42:3). This is precisely the opposite of the Mohican liturgy. Far from destroying a perfectly good sapling, Jesus will quietly care for the bruised reed.

Theologian James Alison quips, "When people tell me that they find Mass boring, I want to say to them: it's supposed to be boring, or at least seriously underwhelming. It's a long term education in becoming un-excited, since only that will enable us to dwell in a quiet bliss . . . which increases our attention, our presence and our appreciation for what is around us."[34]

To the extent people carry pagan expectations and sensibilities with them into Mass, they will be bored. At Mass, they can find it difficult to leave the world of noise,

---

[33] James Fennimore Cooper, *The Last of the Mohicans* (New York: Bantan Books, 1989, orig. 1826), 340.
[34] James Alison. A talk given at Weston Jesuit School of Theology, Cambridge, Mass., on 20 November 2003, originally given at the Ceiliúradh, Christ Church Cathedral, Dublin, in June. It may be found online at 2003.http://www.jamesalison.co.uk/texts/eng13.html

the over-stimulated world of excitement, where peace itself is considered boring.

Flannery O'Connor, the late Catholic Southern author, wrote that, "In contrast to the pious language of the faithful, the liturgy is beautifully flat."[35] By "pious language of the faithful," I believe she had in mind the overwrought, emotional, self-pitying language of some devotionals and the language of those televangelists who passionately dazzle their audiences.

Catholic liturgies, on the other hand, aim at a type of clear-eyed reverence that enables worshipers to perceive their surroundings correctly. If people find themselves bored at Mass, they should stick with it. It means that they're beginning to leave the secular liturgies of this world behind. Boredom at Mass can be a redemptive penance, a saving purgation, which, if endured, can lead to better things.

One might liken the situation to a boy who attends a concert by the Cleveland Orchestra. As it becomes evident to him that no one will crash a guitar on the stage floor against a backdrop of exploding fireworks, the boy may fidget in boredom. If he resigns himself to the experience and fights through the boredom, eventually he may find a transformation taking place. He may learn to tolerate the calmer stretches of music that prepare him to listen correctly to "the good parts." He may eventually become uplifted by the music in ways that he would never have thought possible.

The Mass offers an analogous experience.

---

[35] Flannery O'Connor, *The Habit of Being*, ed. Sally Fitzgerald (New York: Farrar, Straus and Giroux, 1979), 93.

Why is Mass boring? That's like asking why solemnity is boring, or why peace is boring. Ask a passenger who has just endured an exciting airplane ride, complete with spilled beverages, oxygen masks hanging from the ceiling, and a near fatal accident whether the ensuing peace of his living room is "boring." He will find his living-room peace profound and joyful. He will also experience a newfound appreciation for his loved ones.

Why do people need peril to appreciate peace? Why can't people go straightaway to the experience of peace? The Mass tries to educate us into such an experience of joyful peace and appreciation. Of course, the Catholic has moments of passionate excitement in life, but a joyful peace should pervade those experiences. It should affect both the highs and the lows in a Catholic's life.

These observations of course do not excuse those who make Mass boring to even saintly congregations. The boring homily, the priest who mumbles through the prayers, the insertion of foreign elements to hold the people's attention, poor use of liturgical space, dreadful music and the like can interfere with the serene and powerful vision the Mass contains.

Ultimately, we need to be able to enter into the world of the sober but passionate Christ. He offers a peaceful and joyful engagement with his surroundings that ushers in the Kingdom of God, something so valuable he endured the passion of the cross to achieve it for us. Because of Mass, we should be able to take a good, sober, appreciative look at one another, our creation, and the impact that God is having in our lives.

Chapter 26

Growing a Fruitful Lent

by Rev. Andrew B Turner

When we journey through the Season of Lent, we commonly evaluate our "success" in the penances or practices we have chosen to personally observe during the forty days. We often look to Scripture for guidance; however, the Sacred Word provides conflicting advice on this particular question. Certain passages inform us that spiritual accomplishments require both hard work and planning (i.e. Prov. 21:5), and yet others confirm that faithfulness is all that is necessary (i.e. Mk. 5:36).

Many of us choose a particular spiritual practice or devotion for Lent (praying daily for a certain amount of time, fasting from a particular food, donating a certain amount of money, etc.). While these are admirable objectives, we frequently quantify our success solely on our own behavior without leaving room for God's action.

In contrast, Blessed Mother Teresa of Calcutta tells us that "God does not require that we be successful, only that we be faithful." From these words, we infer that faithfulness, orthodoxy in our beliefs and trust in God are the primary factors. While there is truth in this, it can often overlook the concrete call to prayer, fasting and almsgiving that structure the visible marks of discipleship.

Our interior disposition should manifest itself in visible, tangible actions, just as our external performance should reflect our interior disposition.

The book *Center Church* by Pastor Tim Keller proposes a middle ground between measurable achievements and interior faithfulness: fruitfulness.[36] Keller compares Jesus' command to the disciples to "bear much fruit" (Jn. 15:8) to the situation of a farmer. While the farmer is effective in performing the skills necessary for eventual harvest, he must also recognize the success of the farm is also credited to factors outside of his control (quality of the soil, the quality of the seed, the weather, etc.). Just as these conditions can affect farm production, the fruitfulness of our Lenten journey is dependent not only on our action and disposition, but also on the extent to which God blesses and multiplies our efforts.

From the very beginning, everything was created to be fruitful (Gen. 1:28). Saint Paul calls all of us to have the "fruits" of a good character: "love, joy, peace, patience, kindness, generosity, faithfulness, gentleness and self-control" (Gal. 5:22). He also reminds us to manifest good deeds, for example, contributions to the poor (Rom. 15:28). His words remind us to produce perceptible signs of God's presence in our world. Our Lenten practices should lead others to pause, to wonder and to give praise to God. More than just religious rituals and activities, the mark of a fruitful Christian during Lent should be both transformative within as well as observable by all.

---

[36] Tim Keller, *Center Church* (Peabody, MA: Zondervan, 2012).

By this message, I want to encourage all who struggle to evaluate their spiritual growth during the season of Lent. We are all reminded that it is not just a matter of how faithful we are, how many prayers we recite, or how much money we donate. We need to ask what practical actions we can perform each day, however small, that will allow God's abundant love and mercy to be shown to others in our world. Just as in a farm, a "successful" Lent can only be measured by the growth of the fruit and the abundance of the harvest.

Chapter 27

Eucharistic Transformation: "I Am a Living Monstrance"

by Rev. Michael Woost

"He comes within me; by his presence I am a living Monstrance!"[37] Imagine hearing these words after Sunday Mass. Imagine that they were spoken by a member of your community, announced within a group of people gathered in conversation following the celebration of the Eucharist.   Given the context, this person is obviously saying something about herself in relation to Christ whose Body and Blood she has just received. Imagine how you might react to such a pronouncement made by another.

Some of us might well react with startled astonishment, amazed by the boldness of the proclamation.   Others might be left questioning and confused. Why would she say such a thing? Some might be tempted to correct, assuming that the explicit identification of the speaker with the sacred liturgical vessel used for Eucharistic Adoration must be in error. Still others might find themselves abandoning their usual

---

[37] Thérèse of the Child Jesus and the Holy Face, "My Desires Near Jesus Hidden in His Prison of Love," in *The Poetry of Saint Thérèse of Lisieux*, trans. Donald Kinney (Washington, D.C.: ICS Publications, 1996), 134.

hasty exit from church in order to be drawn into the gathering, if only to listen.

These words belong to a woman who died more than a hundred years ago. In popular piety, she is remembered as "the Little Flower"—a saint of Carmel and a Doctor of the Church.

Two years before her death in 1897, St. Thérèse of the Child Jesus and the Holy Face wrote a poem for a member of her Carmelite community in Lisieux. Entitled, "My Desires Near Jesus Hidden in His Prison of Love," the poem expresses some of Thérèse's thoughts on the Eucharist. Although it is central to her spiritual life, Thérèse never collected her reflections on the Eucharist into any kind of systematic treatise. Most of her teachings on the Eucharist are scattered throughout her works, including sixteen of her sixty-two poems.

When Thérèse does speak about the Eucharist, drawing on a major theme of Carmelite spirituality, she describes it as the sacrament of transforming union. The Triune God transforms the bread and wine into the Body and Blood of Christ so that through our participation in the Eucharist we may be transformed. God's intent is to share the fullness of God's life with us, inviting us into an ever deepening union of love with Love. It is this union with Divine Love that transforms us, conforming us to Christ. Typically, Thérèse's poetic references to the Eucharist emphasize this affect on those who desire to be incorporated into the Eucharistic Lord. Her ultimate desire is to live the life of transforming union with her Beloved.

Although her poem discloses the influence of nineteenth century spirituality (e.g., referring to the tabernacle as "the prison" of the Eucharist), Thérèse also assaults the boundaries of popular Eucharistic piety. As she expresses what seems like envy over how near the tabernacle, the tabernacle key, the sanctuary light, the altar stone, the corporal, the paten, the chalice, and the altar are to the Eucharistic Jesus, Thérèse declares that she is of greater value to Christ than these objects, regardless of their significance to the Church's liturgical rites. Not only is she more valuable, but she is also closer to Christ in a manner that is living, conscious, and participatory. No key is needed; her faith opens the door of the tabernacle. Unlike the sanctuary light, she burns with the mystery that is the fire of God's love by which she will inflame others for Jesus. As near as the Eucharistic Lord is to the paten upon which "Jesus comes to rest," Thérèse proclaims: "He comes within me; by his presence I am a living Monstrance!"[38]

This last statement alone warrants further reflection from us. Thérèse deliberately chooses the Monstrance, rather than the tabernacle, as the image by which she describes her union with Christ. Why? Her poem provides no explanation, but her life does. She was not content to have her Beloved hidden within her, as the Eucharist is in the tabernacle. She wanted Christ to be seen—in her words, her actions, her attitudes, her relationships, her ministry, her joys, and her sorrows. Joined to Christ in an ever deepening union through her reception of His Body and Blood, her ongoing transformation in Him continually calls her to witness to

---

[38] *Ibid.*

His Real Presence through, with, and in every aspect of her life.

United to Christ Jesus, she boldly proclaims: " . . . I am a living Monstrance." Desiring only to make Him known, she concludes her poem by exclaiming: "Deign to transform me into You!"[39]

---

[39] *Ibid.*, 135.

Chapter 28

When Eucharist Is Denied

by Rev. Gerald J. Bednar

In Dostoyevsky's *Brothers Karamazov*, an elder comments, "If anything . . . transforms the criminal, it is only the law of Christ speaking in his conscience." Therefore, the Church ". . . does not excommunicate him but simply persists in fatherly exhortation of him."[40]

The elder's statement more accurately describes the Catholic position than most people realize. People are denied Communion in a wide variety of cases even though they may long for the sacrament. Instances range from people who are excommunicated after procuring an abortion, to couples who are not excommunicated but find themselves unable to receive Communion because they married outside the Church, to Protestant spouses who cannot receive Communion even though they pray alongside their Catholic families at Mass.

How should we treat the denial of Communion to these people theologically?

---

[40] Fyodor Dostoevsky, *The Brothers Karamazov*, trans. C. Garnett (New York: The Modern Library, 1950), 72-73.

No one can exclude anyone from Christ's love. No one can exclude anyone from the Church's love either. As the medieval theologian William of Auvergne suggests, the Church never desires to cut off anyone from interior communion with the Lord. The denial of the Eucharist and excommunication are intended to be medicinal. William observed that in some cases excommunication might prompt more patience and humility than continued communion would.[41] As Saint Bonaventure claimed, "No one can be . . . excluded from the communion of love as long as he lives on earth. Excommunication is not such an exclusion."[42]

The denial of the Eucharist does not imply that the excluded are personally unwelcome or have absolutely no place with the communicants of the Church. Excommunication implies that a public irregularity needs to be addressed and rectified in order for the Church and for the excluded to be who they are called to be before Christ. It makes no final judgment on the internal state of conscience of the excluded person. The denial of Communion addresses external behavior, not a person's subjective state of grace. Therefore, excommunication does not necessarily imply that the excluded are not going to heaven. In fact, the Church's act of excluding people from Communion is part of an effort to ensure their salvation. How so?

Eucharistic communion in the Catholic Church implies a unity of mind and heart. A person's relationship

---

[41] Quoted in Joseph Ratzinger (Benedict XVI), *Behold the Pierced One: An Approach to Spiritual Christology* (San Francisco: Ignatius Press, 1986), 95.
[42] *Ibid.*, 96.

to others directly affects his relationship to Jesus. The two cannot be separated (Mt. 25). Unity of mind implies that the communicants believe in the core holdings of the Church, including the real presence of Jesus in the sacrament. If the Church were to allow simply all comers to Communion regardless of their beliefs, it would reduce the sacrament to an empty, superficial ritual. It would not signify even a desire for unity since everyone would be left in the isolation of his or her own thoughts, undisturbed by the thoughts of others. Such is not communion.

Communion also implies a unity of heart. Even Catholics, otherwise in good standing with the Church, cannot receive Communion if they are conscious of unconfessed and unrepented mortal sin.

In all cases, exclusion from Communion is intended as an incentive, a medicine, to those who need to address serious issues in their lives. Although they may enjoy a subjective union with Jesus, they also live in an anomalous situation that contradicts that union. For example, many of our Protestant brothers and sisters live fine, exemplary lives. But the Lord has asked that "all may be one." Our continued separation constitutes a scandal that urgently needs repair. Denial of Communion is an act that insists that serious work remains to be done to achieve that unity, especially in the areas of doctrine and church governance.

Exclusion from the Eucharist always looks forward to a deeper union with the excluded. At times this means that the Catholic Church must recognize its own misdeeds. For example, in its agreement with Lutherans on the doctrine of justification, it admitted that Church leaders had at times added unnecessarily to the division.

The Joint Declaration represents an enormous step towards greater unity.

Occasionally, the medicinal effect of the denial of Communion will result in couples having their marriages validated—sometimes an easy exercise, and sometimes quite difficult, but always a positive response to the Lord's call for deeper unity.

The Church needs to express more explicitly its deep solidarity with those who desire the Eucharist but cannot receive it—especially to avoid the impression that excommunication simply rejects people. Cardinal Ratzinger has noted that St. Augustine, at the end of his life, "excommunicated himself," and began public penance. Denying himself Communion, "He wanted to meet his Lord in the humility of those who hunger and thirst for righteousness."[43] The future Pope Benedict then declared that perhaps the whole Church ought to fast from the Eucharist in recognition of its fundamental solidarity with all people who yearn for the Sacrament but cannot receive it. He suggests that Good Friday might be an appropriate time during which all people are denied the Eucharist since Mass is not permitted on that day anyway.[44]

Theologically Dostoevsky's elder had a point. The denial of Communion should look more like motherly exhortation than rejection. Perhaps we need to do more to make it appear that way.

---

[43] *Ibid.,* 97.
[44] *Ibid.,* 97.

Chapter 29

The Faithfulness of Christ to His Bride, the Church

by Rev. Mark Hollis

As followers of Jesus, we Christians believe that marriage is a Sacrament. One simple definition presents a sacrament as a visible sign of an invisible reality. Think about that definition for a moment or two. Doesn't each sacrament point to something "beyond" what is seen?

What is the "visible sign" of the sacrament of marriage? This sacrament is unique within the Catholic Church. The bride and groom are the actual ministers of the sacrament. The priest, deacon or bishop, as official witnesses of the Church, each can receive the statement of intention from the bride and groom through a series of questions regarding their free entrance into the sacrament, their intention to love and honor each other as man and wife for the rest of their lives, and their intention to accept children lovingly from God, bringing them up according to the law of Christ and his Church. At that point, the bride and groom give their full consent by the pronouncement of their wedding vows. They declare before God and the Christian community that they intend their love to be a free, total, faithful and fruitful commitment.

The next logical question: "What is the invisible reality to which the Sacrament of Matrimony points?" The answer to that question is where the idea of Mystery comes into focus. The union of a Christian man and woman in the

Sacrament of Matrimony is so sacred and so holy that it mirrors, and, at the same time, points to, the union of Christ, the Bridegroom, and his Bride, the Church.

In order to understand Christian marriage, we first have to come to know more about how Christ loves the Church (i.e., His People). St. John Paul II, in his Theology of the Body catechetical instructions (1979-84), tells us that the love Jesus has for the Church is free, total, faithful and fruitful.

The love is free. No one forced Jesus to mount the wood of the Cross and die for us. He did that out of His love for all of humanity. In the Fourth Gospel, He plainly says, "The Father loves me for this: that I lay down my life to take it up again. No one takes it from me; I lay it down freely. I have power to lay it down, and I have power to take it up again" (Jn. 10:17-18).

Therefore, in Christian marriage, the type of love that a husband and wife have for each other should reflect the "self-donation" that Jesus made for the Church; and that love can be described as "sacrificial" in nature. Christian husbands and wives, then, should not take from the other spouse, but rather give themselves freely to each other as Christ gave Himself to us.

The love is total. The self-donation of Jesus was not something partial or incomplete. Quite the contrary is true. Again, in John's Gospel, Jesus prays to the Father, "Just as all that belongs to me is yours, so all that belongs to you is mine" (Jn. 17:10).

If marriage is a covenant, that is, an exchange of persons based on love, then that exchange of gift to the other must not be partial, but rather total. Once again, we see how Christian marriage should reflect the totality of Christ's gift of Himself to His Bride, the Church.

114

The love is faithful. We continue to look at Jesus on the Cross and His absolute fidelity to His Father. In St. Matthew's Gospel, the chief priests, the scribes and the elders jeered at Jesus saying, "He saved others but he cannot save himself. . . . Let's see him come down from that cross and then we will believe in Him" (Mt. 27: 41, 42b). That type of occurrence would almost appear to have a theatrical overtone to it. That was not the way of Jesus. Rather, his last words from the Cross were, "Father, into your hands I commend my spirit" (Lk. 23:46).

The vows made during the celebration of the Sacrament of Matrimony again call to mind the fidelity of Jesus. The bride and groom pledge their fidelity to each other as they each say, "I will love you and honor you all the days of my life."

The love is fruitful. What was the result of the self-donation of Christ? Nothing less than the salvation of the world. In the section of St. John's Gospel called the "Bread of Life Discourse," we hear these words of Jesus, "I am the living bread come down from heaven. If anyone eats this bread he shall live forever; the bread I will give is my flesh for the life of the world" (Jn. 6:51).

In a parallel manner, the "fruitfulness" of marriage is found in the willingness of the couple to accept the gift of children. Jesus gave of Himself for others, for the life of the world. In the first Preface for the Celebration of Marriage, the priest prays, "By your providence and grace, O Lord, you accomplish the wonder of this twofold design: that, while the birth of children brings beauty to the world, their rebirth in Baptism gives increase to the Church, through Christ our Lord."[45]

---

[45] *Roman Missal*, third edition, trans. International Committee on English in the Liturgy Corp. (New Jersey: Catholic Book Publishing Co., 2011), 1026.

In this reflection on the Sacrament of Matrimony, we see the holiness of this vocation and, of course, the importance of proper preparation for such a lifetime commitment that will, with God's grace, continue throughout the years. The Church is deeply grateful to all those who have committed themselves in this holy sacrament. By their love for each other, they are living signs of how Christ loves His Bride the Church.

Section VI

Life, Death and Morals Along the Way

Chapter 30

Keeping Our Gardens Tidy:
Sexual Misconduct in the Military

by Rev. Gerald J. Bednar, Ph.D.

W hen the former Secretary-General of the United Nations, Dag Hammarskjold, died in 1961, he left behind a sketchbook of reflections called *Markings*. In that book, Hammarskjold observes,

> You cannot play with the animal in you without becoming wholly animal, play with falsehood without forfeiting your right to truth, play with cruelty without losing your sensitivity of mind. He who wants to keep his garden tidy doesn't reserve a plot for weeds.[46]

This stunning account of integrity describes an often ignored factor in the recent controversy surrounding sexual misconduct in the military. Let me explain.

During the past several years, the press has increasingly reported on the anti-woman sentiment that

---

[46] Dag Hammarskjold, *Markings* (New York: Doubleday, 1964), 9.

exists in the armed services. Despite the Defense Department's zero tolerance policy, it seems that sexual harassment charges and sexual assaults have grown over the years. The news first hit the front pages concerning a Naval aviation convention in 1991. The problem has only grown worse.

In the meantime, some commentators claim that the basic culture of the military has not changed much at all. Anyone who has been to boot camp can recall marching cadences set to various "Jody calls" that offended against sexual propriety. Those verses that kept everyone in step at times contained lyrics designed to raise the bravado and lower the inhibitions of everyone in the platoon. While many of the Jody calls carried humorous punch lines, everyone knew that they were skating past the edge of propriety.

And that was the point. Every infantryman had to become comfortable skating past the edge of propriety because killing an enemy is not polite—even less polite than a risqué Jody call. I remember years ago at Fort Dix, when our Drill Sergeant introduced us to the bayonet. He drew the blade from its scabbard, looked us in the eye, and declared, "This is a bayonet. You don't take it out of its scabbard to open a can of peas. You don't take it out of its scabbard to open a letter. You take it out of its scabbard because you're going to stick somebody with it." Utter silence. He was, after all, preparing us for combat.

"Thou shalt not kill" is a very direct commandment, and one of the most difficult to obey. Over the years, thinkers have devised exceptions to that commandment. Even the *Catechism* recognizes that self-defense can be an excuse to kill in certain circumstances

(*CCC* 2263, 2308). Nevertheless, the Church much prefers nonviolent ways as reflected in the life of Christ. Even though a given action may be excusable, it does not necessarily follow that it is Christian. Killing in self-defense at times may not be blameworthy, but neither is it particularly Christian.   Nor is it a situation to be encouraged. Killing in self-defense is not at the bottom of the Christian bag of tricks. It is found in an altogether different bag.

Recently more and more people have begun to question the wisdom of various "stand-your-ground" laws. This sentiment resonates with Christian sensibilities. The Lord's commandment is, after all, disarmingly simple. The commandment is not "Thou shalt not *murder*," but "Thou shalt not *kill*." Commentators admit that, as originally used in the Fifth Commandment, the Hebrew word, *rasah*, meant killing, regardless of the motivation. Only later reflection inserted various exceptions that began to limit the word "kill" to mean "murder." Perhaps the earlier reading was right. Jesus seemed to think so. After all, his life and teaching brought that insight much more fully into focus.

There is no "honorable" killing for Christians in the New Testament. Jesus never suggested that we could kill in certain circumstances. In fact, he encouraged the opposite ("But I say to you, offer no resistance to one who is evil. When someone strikes you on the right cheek, turn the other to him as well," Mt. 5:39). He not only commanded the opposite of self-defense, he actually modeled it in his life. If ever there were a person who had a perfect claim to self-defense, it was Jesus; yet he forgave his persecutors and did not fight them.   In Dag

Hammarskjold's terms, Jesus did not reserve a plot for weeds. He did not kill.

One military leader thought he could focus the energy of his young, athletic, virile troops only in positive ways, as if he could harness that energy to kill, but avoid all other improprieties. Good luck. That energy already has spilled over its banks, and there is no telling what other areas it may flood as well. A soldier's ability to compartmentalize his experience no doubt can help, but the act of killing nonetheless compromises his humanity at a fundamental level.

Our troops need spiritual support to deal with this difficult situation. God bless our military chaplains who help our soldiers face this dilemma each day. It cannot be easy. I wish I had a good alternative that would make armed forces and police departments unnecessary, but their activities do furnish a needed peace of sorts, even if it isn't the peace of God's Kingdom.

Nevertheless, Dag Hammarskjold was right. You can't expect a young man to reserve a plot for killing, and expect those weeds to stay put. His observation, of course, does not excuse sexual misconduct. It only offers one sad explanation for it. War, whether it is considered necessary or not, even whether it can be considered "just" or not, is never a Christian solution. It sets up combatants for all sorts of failures—sexual harassment being one of them.

If only we could think of another way.

Chapter 31

Is "Celibacy" the New "Chastity"?

By Rev. Mark S. Ott

Prince Amukamara is a real life prince (the son of a Nigerian village chief), and a starting cornerback for the NFL's New York Giants. From what I've read about him, he is also a devout Catholic who is comfortable witnessing his faith. This fact has led some people, he playfully notes, to refer to him as the "black Tim Tebow."

In a September 18, 2013 article about their city's faith-filled footballer, New York CBS affiliate TV channel 2 posted on its website that Amukamara, ". . . never drinks alcohol, and is committed to staying celibate." When I first read this line, I was intrigued that someone playing in the NFL would take a religious vow to remain unmarried so that he could commit his life to loving service for God's Kingdom. What a unique and powerful witness that would be!

Reading on, however, a direct quote from Amukamara later in the article revealed that Channel 2 was perhaps confused in their earlier description. "I told my fiancée," he noted, "that I'll probably take my first drink at my bachelor party." It turns out Amukamara is not committed to "staying celibate" after all. He is committed to staying *chaste.*

Please don't mistake my making this distinction as a critique of Prince Amukamara. By all accounts, he seems like a great guy and a sincere man of faith. (In fact, Mr. Amukamara, is there any chance I can book you to come and speak to the kids in my youth group?!) I make this distinction, rather, to point out the mistaken word choice made by the writer from Channel 2. This mistake is becoming so common in the popular media, in fact, that I wonder if it has gone beyond the category of "mistake" to become more of a "social agenda."

Throughout Christian history, celibacy has always been the discipline of a relative few. Jesus and Paul were celibate, but Peter and most of Jesus' other followers were not. The celibate life is meant to prophetically draw our minds to contemplate heavenly life, in which we ". . . neither marry nor are given in marriage" (cf. Mk. 12:25). The *Catechism* describes celibacy especially as an evangelical counsel practiced by those in consecrated religious life (cf. *CCC* 915 f.), and by the ordained clergy. They remain celibate ". . . for the sake of the kingdom of heaven," consecrating themselves ". . . with undivided heart to the Lord," so that they can ". . . give themselves entirely to God and to men." When it is undertaken with a joyous heart, ". . . celibacy radiantly proclaims the Reign of God" (*CCC* 1579). But celibacy is not designed to be practiced by everyone, nor even by the majority of Christians. If it were, then Catholicism would be gone in a generation.

Chastity, on the other hand, *is* meant for everyone. It is a *virtue* by which all people come to master and give joyful expression to the powers of life and love that constantly well up within us (cf. *CCC* 2337-2379). The specific expression each person gives to these powers corresponds to his or her state in life. Married people live in "conjugal chastity," uniquely sharing their powers of life and love though sexual intimacy, culminating in healthy family life. Priests and consecrated religious live in "celibate chastity," as described in the paragraph above. And single people live in "continent chastity," forming profound bonds of friendship, spiritual communion, and solidarity with others in the human family.

The virtue of chastity works to correct the *vice* of lust, which distorts and even suppresses the powers of life and love within us. Masturbation, fornication, and adultery fall far short of expressing the kind of selfless love that God calls us to offer. Jesus warned us that such dark desires from deep within are ultimately harmful to us (cf. Mt. 15:19-20). St. Paul consistently counseled his various communities to avoid sexual immorality (in Greek, *porneia*) because of its destructive effects on both the individual and the community (cf. Rom 13:9-10; 1 Cor. 6:18; 2 Cor. 12:21; Gal. 5:9; Eph. 5:3; Col 3:5; 1 Thes. 4:3). From the very beginning, reliance on God's grace to turn away from lust and to live in chastity has been one of the hallmarks of the Christian approach to life. Chastity is, for Christians, the *normal* way to live.

But the secular culture around us does not seem to regard chastity as normal at all. For the surrounding culture, sexual promiscuity is becoming more and more the norm. So much so, in fact, that it seems we are subtly losing the terms "promiscuity" and "chastity" from the popular vocabulary. In popular culture, people now expect that everyone will have premarital sexual encounters.

According to this view, one is only considered promiscuous (i.e., lacking in virtue) if he or she surpasses a certain *arbitrary number* of such encounters. In a context where this is the norm, the concept of chastity no longer has any meaning, so it is no longer used. Instead, people popularly (but mistakenly) refer to those who choose to abstain from sex for a period of time as "celibate." But celibacy defined in *this* way is no virtue at all, much less a sign of the Reign of God. At best, it's just a quirky, boutique, hipster trend that a few people might find to be intermittently helpful.

As baptized Christian prophets, let us challenge one another to reclaim and proclaim the beautiful truth we find in the chaste life. Let us commit ourselves to reflect deeply on the profound insights into the meaning of human sexuality that we can find in Scripture, the Catechism, and Blessed John Paul's "Theology of the Body." Let us internalize these insights, so that we can better explain to ourselves, our children, and our communities that chastity is not a "no" to sexuality, but the most profound "yes" to the powers of life and love with which God has blessed us.

Chapter 32

Is the Church Against
Stem Cell Research?

by Rev. Joseph Koopman

An unfortunate caricature that is often perpetuated in our modern world is that the Catholic Church is an enemy of scientific and technological progress, particular in the realm of bio-medicine. Often citing the controversy regarding the Church and Galileo, many critics contend that the Church continues to remain resistant to scientific and medical breakthroughs that have the potential to improve the lives of millions of people. Among these breakthroughs that the Church supposedly opposes and stifles is that of stem cell research, which holds great promise in how we may be able to treat diseases and illness in the future.

Are these criticisms of the Church true? Is the Church truly against stem cell research?

Before answering these questions, it would be helpful to offer a very brief explanation of the biology (and potential benefit) behind stem cell research. As adult humans, the vast majority of the cells that make up our bodies are called 'somatic cells,' which are differentiated cells—namely, they are *particular* cells, such as skin cells, nerve cells, blood cells, etc. Stem cells, on the other hand, differ from these cells in that they are 'pluripotent,' which means that they have potential to differentiate into a variety of different cells. This characteristic of 'pluripotency,' along with stem cells' prolonged capability of multiplying themselves in this state, have intrigued scientist and researchers, who see the potential of harnessing these cells in order to treat many types of diseases. Indeed, the hopes of 'regenerative medicine' rest on the ability of stem cells to help promote healing and cell growth in damaged cells.

Considering the great potential that stem cell research can offer medicine, we move to the important question: Where do we obtain these stem cells? The answer to this question is critical, since it undergirds the Church's moral response to stem cell research. Whereas stem cells can be found in umbilical cords, in some adult tissue (such as bone marrow), much focus has been on embryonic stem cells. Because stem cells are abundant in early embryonic life, many have proposed utilizing embryonic stem cells for research and development. Such use, however, almost always involves the deliberate destruction of the embryo, since this is the only way in which embryonic stem cells can be harvested. Because of this destruction of early unborn life, the Church has voiced strong opposition to embryonic stem cell research. The embryo is not a *potential* person; the embryo is an actual person, created in the image and likeness of God, and worthy of dignity and respect. Just as human beings go through many stages after they are born (infancy, childhood, pubescence, end of life, etc.), so the stage of 'embryo' is an early stage of a particular human being, whose life is inviolable. As the Church teaches, "The obtaining of stem cells from a living human embryo. . .

invariably causes the death of the embryo and is consequently gravely illicit: research, in such cases, irrespective of efficacious therapeutic results, is not truly at the service of humanity. In fact, this research advances through the suppression of human lives that are equal in dignity to the lives of other human individuals and to the lives of the researchers themselves." (*Dignitas Personae*, no. 32).

While the Church is firm in its opposition to embryonic stem cell research, the exact *opposite* can be said of adult stem cell research (or research that utilizes stem cells not harvested from living embryos). As *Dignitas Personae* states, "Research initiatives involving the use of adult stem cells, since they do not present ethical problems, should be *encouraged and supported*." (no. 32, emphasis added) Thus, while it is true that the Church opposes *embryonic* stem cell research, the Church actually encourages *adult* stem research, namely because it does not involve the destruction of human life, while at the same time offering great promise in medical advancement respecting human dignity. The extent of the Church's support for adult stem research can be seen in the recent unprecedented collaboration of the Vatican's Pontifical Council for Culture with a biotech firm in promoting advancements of stem cell research, including an investment of one million dollars in the partnership.

What makes the Church's support of adult stem research all the more exciting is the genuine advancements made in the field. As opposed to embryonic stem cell research that, while receiving widespread support from the media and the current presidential administration, *has not produced any substantial therapeutic advancements*, adult stem research has done the contrary. There are dozens of current therapies being offered and developed through adult stem research that offer the most hopeful prospects in terms of regenerative medicine. Furthermore, current bio-medical advances in the field of adult stem research have made further progress all the more encouraging. The 2012 Nobel Prize for Physiology and Medicine was awarded to two scientists, Shinya Yamanaka and John Gurdon, whose breakthrough work centers on 'induced pluripotent stem cells' (iPS). These iPS cells, which have the same properties of embryonic stem cells, are derived from adult somatic cells which, genetically manipulated, can take on the qualities of stem cells, with even greater potential in terms of regenerative medicine.

The Church's active support of such research gives witness to its commitment to authentic human progress and flourishing, which always upholds the inherent dignity of the human person.

Chapter 33

End of Life Moral Issues

by Rev. Joseph Koopman

During the month of October, as has been the case for the past forty years, Catholics in the United States are invited to recommit themselves to witnessing to the sanctity of human life in what has been called 'Respect Life Month.' In defending what the *Catechism of the Catholic Church* calls ". . . the transcendent dignity of man" (*CCC* 1929), the Church focuses our concern primarily on beginning-of-life and end-of-life issues in response to disturbing trends in our culture that deny and attack the dignity of some of the most vulnerable in our community. In light of this invitation, we should examine the Church's teaching on end of life issues. In doing so, it becomes clear that, in defense of the transcendent dignity of every human person, the Church's teaching offers an important counter-balance to extreme views that exist today in regards to issues that surround the end of life.

Arguably the most disturbing and prevalent view that the Church seeks to counter is one that bases the dignity of the human person merely on "usefulness" or "quality." This position, which could be called "utilitarian," bases the "worth" of human life on how useful a person is, or on how 'functional' they are. As Blessed John Paul II explains in his encyclical *Evangelium Vitae*, the Christian understanding of the dignity of the human person ". . . is replaced by the criterion of efficiency, functionality and usefulness: others are considered not for what they 'are', but for what they 'have, do and produce'" (*EV* 23). For example, if a sick elderly grandparent is a "burden" (whether financially or emotionally) on a family, or if a person in a so called "persistent vegetative state" can no longer function as they did when they were healthy, their "worth" and "dignity" is seen as compromised, thus justifying euthanasia or assisted suicide.

In arguing against this utilitarian view, the Church stands firm in its position that the dignity of the person is *not* dependent on one's quality of life, function, or usefulness; rather, the sanctity of human life is rooted in the fact that all persons are created in the "image of God." As John Paul makes clear, it is *who we are*, not merely *what we can do* or our *quality of life* that establishes our dignity as persons. A diminishment of "quality" or "function" can never take away this dignity. Therefore, not only does the Church fight against the mentality of euthanasia, but also insists that those, ". . . whose lives are diminished or weakened deserve special respect" (*CCC* 2276). As the Church has recently clarified, this respect includes basic human care, including a presumption for artificial nutrition and hydration (i.e., feeding tubes).

While the Church views this utilitarian approach as a great threat to a true understanding of the sanctity of life, the Church's teaching also responds to an opposite extreme, which could be called the "vitalist" approach. This approach holds that we must do everything in our power, including procedures and treatments that are excessive and burdensome, to prolong life in end of life situations.

What often underlies this position is an assumption that life here on earth is the only good, and thus must be prolonged at all costs. The Church's teaching counters this assumption with the fact that part of the "transcendent dignity" of the human person is that we are created for eternal communion with God—i.e., we are not ultimately made for this world, but for heaven. Though firmly defending the dignity and sanctity of every person, including those who have diminished capacity because of illness, the Church also upholds the truth that life here on earth is not the end of the story.

In response, then, to a vitalist approach that argues that we should pursue every means necessary to prolong life, the Church offers important balance. As articulated by Pope Pius XII, and in a more recent development by the Vatican, the Church makes the important distinction between ordinary or proportionate treatment and extraordinary or disproportionate treatment. In defining extraordinary or disproportionate treatment, the Church teaches that we are not morally obligated to undergo treatments or procedures that are excessively burdensome, and which offer no reasonable hope of benefit (*CCC* 2278). For example, if an elderly person is extremely ill, and dependent upon a ventilator or a dialysis machine for survival despite the fact that such treatments are excessively burdensome and offer no reasonable hope of recovery (i.e., the person will most likely be on the ventilator permanently), there is no moral obligation to continue those treatments. While such decisions require prayerful and prudent reflection, the Church's position is clear that, in such cases, we are not bound to pursue excessive treatment.

In defending the transcendent dignity of the human person, the Church's teaching on end of life issues challenges us to witness to an important balance: to affirm both the sanctity of human life beyond mere usefulness, and to affirm that our true home is ultimately with God in heaven.

Chapter 34

Bury the Dead!
The Church's Teaching on
Cremation

By Rev. Joseph Koopman

Recently, after offering prayers at a wake, I was a bit surprised to see that the funeral home had set up a display where they were selling a variety of different pieces of jewelry. Upon closer inspection, the pieces for sale (including pendants, bracelets, necklaces, rings, and even key-chains) were not ordinary jewelry; rather, they were all designed to carry bits of cremains, the ashes of a deceased person who had been cremated. As one on-line company advertises, "Along with the rising number of cremations in recent years comes a wide range of options for storing cremated remains and memorializing deceased loved ones. Among those options, cremation jewelry is quickly becoming a favorite choice of survivors who wish to pay tribute to their departed loved ones and hold them forever close at heart."

Grief from losing loved ones is something all of us experience; so too is the desire to remember and to remain close to those who have passed on from this world. The Church acknowledges this, not only in its funeral rites, in every Mass, and its pastoral outreach to the grieving, but in a special way every November.

Yet, while the Church encourages us to pray for and to remember our deceased loved ones, what of this new trend of carrying cremains in jewelry? Or of the practice of keeping the urn of a loved one on our mantles, or scattering their remains in memorable places (such as the ocean, parks, or gardens)? To answer these questions, it would be helpful to briefly explore both the history of the Church's approach to cremation, along with its theology of death and dying.

Cremation was commonplace in the ancient world of early Christianity, particularly in the Roman empire. However, as opposed to cremating the bodies of the deceased, early Christians (following the tradition of Judaism) buried the dead. Part of the reason they chose burial, as opposed to cremation, centers on the importance of the body in our tradition. At the heart of our faith is the great mystery of the Incarnation: that God became flesh in the person of Jesus. Far from insignificant or worthless, our bodies have great importance and dignity. This is the case not only with Christ, but also for all of us. As St. Paul challenges, our bodies are actually temples of the Holy Spirit. Furthermore, the reality of the resurrection highlights the importance of the body. On Easter Sunday morning, Christ did not appear as a ghost to his disciples; rather, his resurrection from the dead was a bodily reality. He ate food with his disciples; and he invited Thomas to place his fingers in his wounds. And just as his resurrection was a bodily resurrection, so also our existence in heaven will also be bodily. As we profess every Sunday during the creed, our belief in the resurrection of the dead is that, at the end of time, all those who have died will be re-united with their glorified bodies. As the Catechism explains, "The 'resurrection of the flesh' (the literal formulation of the Apostles' Creed) means not only that the immortal soul will live on after death, but that even our 'mortal body' will come to life again."

It was because of this belief that, for part of its history, the Church opposed cremation. This opposition centered not on the act of cremating as such, but rather on an accompanying denial of the reality of the bodily resurrection. As cremation became more commonplace in the 20th century, and because people did not intend cremation to be a denial of the resurrection of the dead, the Church lifted the prohibition in 1963 (and promulgated it in the 1983 Code of Canon Law), allowing Catholics to choose cremation.

However, while the Church allows cremation, it still guards against situations where the cremains are not given proper respect. As the Rites state, "the cremated remains of a body should be treated with the same respect given to the human body from which they come." This respect includes a proper burial. As the Rites continue, "The cremated remains should be buried in a grave or entombed in a mausoleum or columbarium. The practice of scattering cremated remains on the sea, from the air, or on the ground, or keeping cremated remains on the home of a relative or friend of the deceased are not the reverent disposition that the Church requires." Reverence for the body, therefore, is the underlying reason the Church opposes the above practices, which would also include distributing ashes to be worn in jewelry. Our bodies, and the remains of our bodies, are not mere objects or commodities; rather, they have dignity that demand respect and reverence.

One last note: while the Church stresses that proper burial is the only practice that upholds the dignity of the body and the reverence owed the body, there are other deeper, spiritual reasons for burial. While it is true that, in our tradition, Christians buried their dead, it is also true that Christians would often return to the place of burial, as to a sacred place, offering their prayers for the dead. This practice continues, as evident in the many Catholic cemeteries throughout our diocese, and our world.

As for my family, we regularly go to the grave of my dad, as a way not only to pray for him, but also to honor him and remember him. Going to this sacred place, where he is buried with dignity and respect, continues to bring us healing from our grief, and renews our hope in the resurrection of the dead.

Chapter 35

Praying for the Dead

by Sr. Mary McCormick, OSU

O n November 2nd of each year, the Church marks the Feast of All Souls. Together with the Feast of All Saints on November 1st, the entire month of November is the month in the church when we remember the dead in a special way in prayer.

When people die, the church intercedes on behalf of the deceased because of its belief that death is not the end and that, "the ties of friendship and affection which knit us as one throughout our lives do not unravel with death," to quote one of the prayers in the *Order of Christian Funerals*. Catholic tradition has developed a theology of life and death as well as a practice of prayer that helps the living to deepen our faith in God's promise.

At the end of the Creed we profess that we believe in ". . . the communion of saints, the forgiveness of sins, the resurrection of the body and life everlasting." Our faith is rooted in the God who created us for eternal life even though our bodies die. God fulfills the promise of eternal life first in the death and resurrection of Jesus who has broken the chains of sin and death. Those who share the faith of the church in the God of Jesus also have a share in this promise.

For those who have lived a virtuous life in Christ and those who receive the sacraments shortly before death the promise of everlasting life seems simple enough and God's gracious reward. But some people die before they are ready, or of a sudden cause, or in an accident. This reality causes us to wonder if God's promise will go unfulfilled.

To pray for the dead presumes that there is a connection between those who have died and the community still living on earth. It also presumes an interim between the moment of death and when one is received into heaven. Catholic doctrine teaches that those who die in the state of grace but who may have unabsolved venial sins or still "owe" some temporal punishment for other sins already forgiven in the past may go through this interim between death and heaven. The church believes that reparation must be made before the soul can enter into heaven. If it is possible that temporal punishment can be remitted in this world, it seems likely that there is also the possibility of purification in the next world. This is what the tradition means by purgatory. It is also important to remember that what I just described as an *interim* is without time or space. At the moment of death one moves beyond time and space into God's eternal present.

The church can come to the help of those who have died through intercessory prayer and through the Eucharist. The *Catechism of the Catholic Church* assures us that all who die in God's grace and friendship, but still imperfectly purified, are assured of salvation; but after death they undergo purification so as to achieve the holiness necessary to enter heaven (cf. *CCC* 1030-31).

There is no explicit doctrine of purgatory in the Scripture, but there are passages that imply the existence of purgatory. One of the earliest is a passage from 2 Maccabees. In an account describing the effort of Judas Maccabeus who takes up a collection for an expiatory sacrifice, the author of Second Maccabees writes, ". . . if he were not expecting the fallen to rise again, it would have been useless and foolish to pray for them in death" (2 Macc. 12:44). Catholicism has taken this passage to refer to the resurrection of the body. It has also been used to express a belief in a sense of solidarity that exists between the living and the dead.

Though there is little Scriptural basis for praying for the dead, because of the death and resurrection of Jesus, the early church Christians began to pray for the dead as early as the second century. By the third century the church developed a custom of praying for the dead during the celebration of the Eucharist. In the Roman Canon there is an explicit mention of the dead and the church prays for the dead. This practice continues in our own day in the prayer of the church, specifically in the Eucharistic prayer and each day in the liturgy of the hours.

That we pray for the dead is a way in which we affirm the union of the church on earth with the communion of saints. Though the dead are separated from life on earth, they are still united with the communion of believers. Moreover, they benefit from the prayers and intercessions of the church on earth. It is a spiritual bond that exists between those still living and those who have died.

During the month of November we remember all those who have died: members of our families and friends, members of our parish communities, and especially those who die alone, lonely, imprisoned, or in acts of violence.

Hearing the Call: Vocations

Chapter 36

The "FEST" and Building a Mission-Focused Church

by Rev. Andrew B Turner

The Book of Proverbs states: "Without a vision the people perish" (29:18). In the core of every person is a desire to live a life of significance, and to be involved in something greater than themselves. Jesus shared a radical vision called the Kingdom of God. It was an infinite revelation involving nothing less than a re-creation of the entire world, one person at a time. This goal, this vision, was the focus and purpose of his life; it was the reason he lived and died.

Our Catholic Church was, and continues to be, challenged to bring this vision of Jesus Christ to life in our world. In response to this task, and to inspire the next generation of young adult leaders, the Catholic Diocese of Cleveland began an event known as "The FEST."

The FEST is a celebration of faith comparable to a diocesan-sized World Youth Day. The day-long event is free and open to all. It typically gathers over 30,000 teens, young adults, families and adults to share the Catholic faith through music, prayer, worship and inspiration.

This event, held on a Sunday in early August, has been successful due largely to the use of the new evangelization mediums of the day. It also leverages the gifts and talents of the intergenerational Catholic participants themselves. The FEST's greatest resource is the creative capacity of those who respond to Christ's call to live out his inspirational mission.

From a Catholic leadership perspective, The FEST focuses on more than empowering people and encouraging them to complete a task, goal or program. Rather, it invites them to a renewal of their baptismal vocation to make disciples. This is accomplished through invitation to more than just a one-day event, but an entire year of prayer, mission experiences, talks, service opportunities, and parish involvement that are connected to The FEST. Jesus tells his disciples, "I have come to set the world on fire and how I wish it were already blazing!" (Lk. 12:49). He asked his disciples to leave their comfortable world behind to follow him. He calls this generation to the same challenge. The FEST has taken up the invitation by being a vision-builder for the future leadership of the Church.

Management theory suggests that when an organization becomes mission-effective and focused on a core vision, there is both an increase in participation and a stronger commitment from its members. This commitment comprises a willingness to exert considerable effort on behalf of the organization as well as a strong desire to support that organization.

While the Church is not a business, she is able to learn from certain business models. In order to live fully the mission of Jesus Christ, the leaders within the Church must present a clear purpose and vision on which Catholics can model their lives. This vision must be alive with the "blazing fire" promised by Christ to his followers.

As Catholics, our invitation to involvement in the life of the Church must reflect Christ's radical call. It is not enough merely to be involved in liturgical roles, Bible studies or sacramental preparation programs. The sign of a dynamic parish is not dependent just on attendance, but on the extent that parishioners are on fire to fulfill the mission. The hope of the Second Vatican Council was a renewal of the Church with the fire of the Spirit and an inspiration for people to live lives as saints and martyrs. The Catholic Diocese continues to pursue this goal through The FEST which invites people to make courageous choices that will build God's Kingdom.

As such, The FEST is more than just a day of Catholic celebration; rather, it serves as a concrete example of evangelization and mission alive in the local community. Each year, the event becomes a renewed entrance point for both active and disconnected Catholics, and a highlight on the calendar for thousands of faithful young adults and families throughout the Diocese.

Chapter 37

A Personal Invitation

by Rev. Michael McCandless

There is one Sunday morning from my youth that will always remain a special memory. I was seventeen years old and a junior at Archbishop Hoban High School. I had just finished serving 7:00 A.M. Mass at Holy Family in Stow where I attended eight years of grade school and where my family and I were permanent fixtures in the fifth row of one of the side sections every Sunday morning. An older married couple approached me at the back of Church where I was standing next to the priest and said, "Michael, we have seen you grow up at this parish. You have served Mass ever since your head barely stuck over the altar. We think you belong on the altar... Have you ever thought of being a priest?"

Ever since that Sunday morning I have *never* forgotten that encounter . . . ever. Although I had thought about priesthood from time to time as I grew up and even pictured myself doing the actions of the priest at Mass, I never discussed priesthood openly with anybody before, except in making a few short comments to my parents from time to time. No one had approached me previously with such directness and sincerity. In fact, I never saw this coming, but it must have been a planned surprise in God's eyes, because he wanted to break into my plans with his plans. This couple was his living voice. In the end, I had thought about priesthood as much as any young Catholic man in high school would naturally consider it, but then I was approached and invited to think about priesthood in a way that every young Catholic man *should* be approached!

What was the result of that Sunday morning conversation? I became *invited*. Priesthood became a *possibility*. I remember asking later on, "Am I supposed to do this, Lord?" I naturally trusted the people around me in Church. This couple and eventually others—my parish priests included—were supporting me and proposing to me what could be God's plan for me. Their voices had impact. I realized that the people of my parish *cared for and desired priests in their lives*. In short, the result was that my dreams and plans were altered. My thought of studying chemistry and engineering, and probably getting married one day (frequently the only vocation a high school student has ever considered), was now in competition with this newly-formed desire for priesthood.

Two years later and after my freshmen year of classes at the University of Akron, I transferred to Borromeo Seminary. The curiosity about priesthood had grown. My prayer was impacted. So much was set in motion after that weekend of receiving the invitation from that brave couple whom I had never met before personally.

A. *"Proactivity," and "Inactivity" and Vocations to the Priesthood*

Every day as an American Church we fight a battle as the underdog. Every day society invites our youth—in fact, all people—to a very money-centered, pleasure-centered, and success-oriented lifestyle. How can I succeed over others? How can I derive the most pleasure from things or people? How can I have what I want, or *more* of what I want? Baptism, holiness, vocation, service, kingdom, altruism, gifts—these are not part of society's pitch, and so must be introduced through another source. Do we see that they must be introduced through us—from you and me? "We are Jesus' hands and feet now", as St. Theresa of Avila wrote. Do we see that, more specifically, a vocation to priesthood or religious life will get easily drowned, crowded out, and be the seed choked by the thorns if we do not give it life or a voice? Ideas may eventually die in the busy-ness of our lives, but invitations include another's—and the Church's—good.

Being proactive is giving life—literally, our time, effort, and attention—to what should live, to what we see as valuable. When we give life to further the kingdom, when we are proactive, when we invite, it is no surprise these values keep on living! Jesus needed but a few loaves and fish; with numerous hearts, minds, and much creativity there are unforeseen and beautiful results to come! There is a direct variable between what we are proactive about in our faith and how our family, our parish, and our diocese will evolve into a small part of the "heavenly Jerusalem"!

The biggest factor—the hinge on which a priestly or religious vocation will grow in reality, or not, in our local Church—rests on whether we are acting, promoting, inviting, and praying in place of being indifferent, of giving no life, nor time, nor attention to this enterprise which so greatly serves and impacts.

B. *Where Can We Plug In?*

We are already blessed to have the Diocesan Seminaries . . . blessed to have the priests who invite others . . . and blessed to have supportive parishioners and families at numerous parishes. We have outstanding vocational support and prayer groups: the Knights of Columbus, the Serrans, the Avilas, the Holy Name Society and our Parents of Priests. We have events like the FEST, where tens of thousands of parishioners gather to celebrate our Catholic faith, attend Reconciliation and Mass, and visit the many priests and religious who make themselves available, and whose contagious smiles tell so much. We also have a shepherd in Bishop Lennon who has personally written about the goodness of this priestly life, who greets the children in the aisle after Masses at the Cathedral, and who hosts annual dinners at the Seminary for the young men of our diocese who sense a calling to the priesthood.

Look for opportunities to invite someone to consider the priesthood. Consider playing a proactive part to encourage our men to the priesthood, and women to the religious life. Do this in your own way or aid the wonderful initiatives already present. More great fruit will be forthcoming! So much can happen by going out of our way to get to the back of church to give that invitation to some special youngster, even just once.

Chapter 38

The Hearts of the Youth: A Garden
by Rev. Michael McCandless

Your love's so strong, I can't recall
What was this thing they called the Fall?
And You walk with me, You never leave,
You're making my heart a garden.

"Garden" by Matt Maher

Matt Maher's lyrical poetry describes with Scriptural allusions the redemptive accompaniment of Jesus Christ who renews us, restoring in our hearts the original garden of love. The desire of the Savior is to prepare the ground and "plant" His word and very life into each of us, hoping for great fruit for the whole world as the result. The lyrics strikingly describe Jesus' activity since His incarnation, but what is worth joyfully celebrating is the *witnessing* of this tending and planting of the garden taking place time and again within our youth and young adults, locally and worldwide.

The well-publicized events of World Youth Day in 2013 had a great impact on the universal Church, and, additionally for us in the Cleveland Diocese, the events of the FEST that took place on our Seminary grounds a few days later. God's desire to make the hearts of our youth and young adults a "garden" for himself was unmistakable in the Spirit's activity for both of these events.

During the Saturday evening Vigil at World Youth Day, Pope Francis prepared a special message for those attending. He spoke to them on the Gospel passage of the sower and the seed, preaching that the field in this parable is not a geographical place, it is our hearts! He described the heart – the destination God seeks to plant Himself within us – as the real ground of our lives, where God's Word will sprout, and the most interior parts of ourselves. It is a place "not of momentary fashions or fads," the Holy Father declared. He described the field of the heart as also a training ground and a construction site; it is where we must exercise our choosing God and His plans consistently, and where His love will begin to be manifested in time and space by its impact on our actions. Pope Francis finished his message by encouraging all those who were with him to be "agents of change," constructing the Church with living stones.

Locally, just a few days after World Youth Day, thousands of youth and young adults gathered for a beautiful day at the FEST. The Diocesan Vocation Office had the privilege of once again offering a "Vocation Village," where numerous religious and priests from within and outside our Diocese gathered to attend, meet with the youth of our diocese, and offer their lives as examples of ongoing commitments and vocations. A very sacred moment of the day was the time of Eucharistic Procession and Adoration where about 1400 youth and young adults gathered to be with Christ in the Blessed Sacrament. This was "holy ground", where beautiful singing, beautiful prayers, and beautiful silence was offered to the Lord. It was an event where Christ was doing much cultivating, I believe. Following the time of adoration was another opportunity for the youth to be encouraged to pray about their vocations and to have time with a priest, sister, or brother.

With so many hearts and ears observably open at these events it is my prayer that there are many who have been touched and many who have sensed more clearly what God has been preparing for some time within them.

The hearts of young people, especially those in high school and college, constantly desire a wide variety of ends. They ultimately do not want, as expressed in Augustine's famous prayer, "...to be outside while God is on the inside." There is a tremendous fire within them; they are indeed a vibrant resource. Their discernment will provide many generations of married couples, strong families, good preaching, sisters and brothers who teach, accompany and counsel, as well as the sacramental services of priests. They want God to plant His plans and desires within them – may we pray that it happens and may we pray the gardens of their hearts beautify everything around us.

Chapter 39

The Path to Ordination: Discernment, Formation, and Grace

By Dr. Edward Kaczuk

E very day, in the halls on the way to and from my office, I pass the pictures of all of the graduates of Saint Mary Seminary who have been ordained to the priesthood. Composite pictures of each class from the year 1932 hang on the walls—1,094 men in all. I know some of these men personally, and their lives of priestly ministry are exemplary. Many others, I am sure, lived lives in faithful service to the Diocese of Cleveland. Others have left the active ministry. Still others unfortunately became implicated in the clergy sexual abuse scandal.

These ever-present pictures led me to reflect frequently on the mystery of the priestly vocation. The Church tells us that there are two inseparable elements in every priestly vocation: the free gift of God and the responsible freedom of the recipient. A call from God to the priesthood is a gift of divine grace, received through the Church and for the service of the Church. In responding to the call of God, the man offers himself freely in love. But the desire to become a priest is not sufficient in itself. No one has a right to receive ordination. As with all the sacraments, the Church has the responsibility to define the necessary requirements for reception. Therefore the Church, the whole community of the faithful, discerns the suitability of one who desires to enter the seminary, accompanies him during his years of formation, and to calls him to orders if he is judged to possess the necessary qualities.

It is the responsibility of those involved in seminary formation to prepare these men as well as possible, and to help them experience priestly ministry as much as possible. My colleagues and I work diligently to recruit worthy men and to form these men into candidates that are holy, healthy and happy. It is a difficult task. We are aided at key points by detailed psychological evaluations of the candidates. As I am involved in the faculty evaluations of the college seminarians, I frequently find myself wondering how I would fair under such scrutiny. I am privileged to witness to the seminarians as a lay married person committed to ministry in the Church. I am often awed by their witness of holiness as they prepare to embrace celibate, priestly and vowed lives in service to the Gospel.

The candidates themselves bear the primary responsibility for their own formation. They must commit themselves to full participation in seminary formation. They must trust the discernment of the Church, their bishop, rector, spiritual director and all who are involved in their formation. They must build a spirit of truth, loyalty and openness that must characterize the personality of one who is called to serve Christ and his Church in the ministerial priesthood.

It strikes me that openness to scrutiny in all aspects of one's life is important for any healthy human being. For instance, from my limited knowledge of sexual abuse, one characteristic of abusers is their ability to compartmentalize. They may lead worthy lives for the most part, but they have this one aspect of their life that is kept separate and secret, not open to scrutiny.

The task of preparing holy priests is also the responsibility of the entire Diocesan Church. Throughout their years at the Seminary, candidates serve in various ministries throughout the Diocese: in hospitals, schools, nursing homes, soup kitchens and parishes. They are evaluated by their supervisors who are priests and deacons, as well as women religious and lay persons. In the third year of a five year graduate program, St. Mary Seminarians spend seven months on internship in a parish. They are evaluated by their pastors and supervisors, the lay pastoral staff and a lay formation board made up of members of the parish community.

By means of the Sacrament of Orders, the Holy Spirit configures the candidate to Jesus Christ in a new and specific way: the priest sacramentally represents Christ, the head, the shepherd and the spouse of the Church. At the same time, the Church ordains men to the priesthood who are human beings, with many of the same strengths and weaknesses as everyone else. While there are criteria and observable behaviors to be met, despite our best efforts, no foolproof method gives assurance that the right men have been called to the priesthood. As in marriage or the raising of children, there are no guaranteed outcomes. St. Thomas Aquinas, one of the greatest minds of the Church, was called 'The Dumb Ox' by his fellow novices— so little insight did they have in what a vocation looks like. Jesus himself chose apostles who betrayed, denied and abandoned him—men few would choose today.

Ultimately, preparing holy priests is the work of the mystery of grace. Grace is at work in every step of the process in both obvious and subtle ways. Often my colleagues and I shake our heads in wonder at small things that have a profound effect in the lives of seminarians. Even a small word of encouragement can go a long way.

And here's the best part. Just as conversion doesn't end with Baptism and love must grow throughout a marriage, priests continue to be formed after ordination. Sixty-eight pictures on those walls are of ordained priests that I have worked with personally. The vast majority, after a year or so in the ministry, come back to the Seminary to visit with eyes shining, extolling the wonders of the priestly life. They continue to grow and learn and be formed by their work among the people of God.

As we, lay and ordained, share the Christian life, we constantly call each other to growth in the life of faith and service that is proper to our vocations. What a great grace, what a great mystery.

Chapter 40

Benchmarks of Priestly Identity

By Rev. Mark Hollis

Many questions arise when Christians consider their vocation in life. Should I marry? Should I remain single? Should I consider the priesthood or religious life? For a man considering a call to the priesthood, five "benchmark identities" or characteristics can help him discern God's will. Christ can be identified as the Beloved Son, Chaste Spouse, Spiritual Father, Spiritual Physician and Head and Shepherd. How can those identities help one to discern a call to the priesthood?

At His Baptism Jesus experienced being the Beloved Son of the Father. At the moment of our Baptism all Christians are incorporated into Christ and become "Children of God." As Jesus is loved by the Father, so are we. For a man discerning a vocation to the priesthood, his heart should gradually become more aware of his own "sonship" and sense that Christ may want to live His priesthood through him.

St. Paul wrote, "Husbands love your wives, as Christ loves the Church" (Eph. 5:25). As Chaste Spouse, Christ offered Himself for His Bride, the Church. Likewise the priest offers the free gift of himself, in love, to the Bride of Christ, the Church. He is to be chaste in body, mind and heart so he can give himself fully to the Church in fidelity and love.

The process of discernment and prayer continues as a man reflects on the priest as Spiritual Father. At Baptism the Father bestows on him the grace of being a beloved son. A man considering the priesthood should desire to give that identity to someone else. The priest as spiritual father begets new sons and daughters for the Church. The priest as father generates and protects the gifts of the Holy Spirit present in God's people. The multiple roles a father exercises in a family are paralleled in the life of the priest. He is to teach and instruct, to correct and forgive. As a father grieves with his family and for them, so too the priest. As a father feeds his family, so too the priest. A simple question a man can ask is, "Do I desire to be a spiritual father?"

As Divine Physician, Jesus conquered sin and death. One particular way the priest extends the healing of Christ the Spiritual Physician is through the sacramental ministry of the Church. In Baptism, a spiritual cleansing and regeneration take place. In the sacrament of Penance, sins are forgiven and life is restored. The Holy Eucharist strengthens us to "fight the good fight" by living the Gospel message while the Anointing of the Sick comforts and consoles. What is necessary to be a spiritual physician? A priest must truly believe that the sacraments are indeed visible signs of invisible realities. As the priest himself has received the healing power of Christ in these sacraments, he needs to "give" what he has received.

Christ is the Head Shepherd of the Church. A priest exercises pastoral authority and pastoral charity in a similar way. He must always remember the words of Jesus, "But if I washed your feet—I who am Teacher and Lord—then you must wash each other's feet. What I did was to give you an example" (Jn. 13: 14-15).

Looking at each of these benchmark identities, it should be more than evident that a call to the sacramental priesthood is a vocation about relationship. Fr. David Toups in *Reclaiming Our Priestly Character* says that, "This relationship is primarily one with God, to continue to grow in knowledge and friendship with Him and serve Him in His people out of love."[47]

In spiritual discernment, personal prayer is of prime importance. Speaking and listening to the Lord are fundamental. To ensure that one is on the right path, spiritual direction is a true blessing in a person's life. To be able to speak to someone about one's prayer and the movements of one's heart can really help an individual see things more clearly and objectively.

These benchmark identities are part of the identity of a diocesan priest. May we pray that the Lord will raise up priests for the Church who are ardent and gentle servants of the Gospel, formed in the image of Christ, the Eternal Priest.

---

[47] David Toups, *Reclaiming Our Priestly Character* (Omaha: Institute for Priestly Formation, 2010).

List of Authors

Rev. Gerald J. Bednar, Ph.D.
Professor of Systematic Theology
Ph.D., 1990, Fordham University
Bronx, New York

Dr. Chad Engelland
Professor of Philosophy
Ph.D., 2005, The Catholic University of America
Washington, D.C.

Rev. Damian J. Ference, Ph.L.
Assistant Professor of Philosophy
Ph.L., 2009, The Catholic University of America
Washington, D.C.

Rev. Mark Hollis, M.Chr.Sp.
Spiritual Director, St. Mary Seminary
Assistant Professor of Pastoral Theology
M.Chr.Sp., 1984, Creighton University
Omaha, Nebraska

Dr. Edward Kaczuk
Professor of Liturgical-Sacramental Theology
Ph.D., 2006, Kent State University
Kent, Ohio

Rev. Joseph M. Koopman, STD
Assistant Professor of Moral Theology
STD, 2009, Accademia Alfonsiana
Rome, Italy

Rev. Mark A. Latcovich, Ph.D.
Professor of Pastoral Theology
Ph.D., 1996, Case Western Reserve University
Cleveland, Ohio

Rev. John F. Loya, M.A.
Assistant Professor of Pastoral Theology
Spiritual Director, Borromeo Seminary
M.A. (Spirituality), 1989, Santa Clara University
Santa Clara, California

Rev. Michael P. McCandless, M.A.
Vocation Director, Diocese of Cleveland
M.A., 2008, St. Mary Seminary and Graduate School of Theology
Cleveland, Ohio

Sr. Mary McCormick, OSU
Professor of Systematic Theology
Ph.D., 2001, Fordham University
Bronx, New York

Rev. Francis J. Moloney, SDB
University Professor of Scripture
St. Mary Seminary Mullen Scholar in Residence, 2013
Australian Catholic University
D.Phil. (Oxon), 1976, Oxford University
Oxford, England

Rev. Mark S. Ott, S.S.L.
Assistant Professor of Sacred Scripture
S.S.L., 2010, Pontifical Biblical Institute
Rome, Italy

Rev. Lawrence A. Tosco, CSJ
Professor of Sacred Scripture
S.S.D., 1983, Pontifical Biblical Institute
Rome, Italy

Rev. Andrew B. Turner, M.A.
Director of Field Education
M.A., 2006, St. Mary Seminary and Graduate School of Theology
Cleveland, Ohio

Rev. Michael G. Woost, S.T.L.
Assistant Professor of Liturgical-Sacramental Theology
S.T.L., 2000, The Catholic University of America
Washington, D.C.